A **DIAMOND** IN THE **ROUGH**

STEVEN VAN BELLEGHEM

Lannoo
Campus

This book was originally published as De ruwe diamant.

D/2023/45/257 – ISBN 978 94 014 9546 2 – NUR 800, 802

Cover design: Karl Demoen
Interior layout design: Karl Demoen
Typesetting and interior layout: Adept vormgeving
Translation: Lynn Butler

LannooCampus Publishers is a subsidiary of Lannoo Publishers, the book and multimedia division of Lannoo Publishers nv.

LannooCampus Publishers
Vaartkom 41 box 01.02
3000 Leuven
Belgium
www.lannoocampus.com

P.O. Box 23202
1100 DS Amsterdam
Netherlands

TABLE OF CONTENTS

INTRO-
DUCTION

The Meteora mountains in northern Greece are unique. Millennia of erosion have resulted in a breath-taking spectacle of high, somewhat rounded peaks, deep valleys and mysterious formations. The Meteora was a highlight of a family road trip across mainland Greece. Ancient Greek Orthodox monasteries are perched atop the peaks and six of them contain active orders of monks and nuns, evoking images of Greek religious life in bygone times.

The architectural beauty of the monasteries and their setting was striking, but the irrepressible marketeer in me was also struck by the poor quality of their souvenir shops. Each of the active monasteries has a shop. On our visit, five of them were devoid of customers. These five offered an identical range of dusty knick-knacks and were staffed by bored salespeople staring listlessly at their mobile phones.

One monastery, Agios Stefanos, presented quite a different scene. There, it was the nuns themselves who ran the shop. They described their products to customers with enthusiasm, proudly rang up sales of homegrown herbs and homemade teas, oils and liqueurs and kept the shop in order. Unsurprisingly, this shop was packed with customers during our visit and few left empty-handed.

WHY WERE THE NUNS MORE SUCCESSFUL THAN THE MONKS?

There are six market players in Meteora. The context of the market is the same for all six. Yet only one of the six shops seemed successful. Why?

At first glance, the answer is simple: the nuns' products were better and, combined with their passion and charm, this gave customers a unique and appealing experience.

But perhaps there was something more at play. They may have had an inspiring leader, skilled at motivating the nuns to take part, or a reward system that motivated the nuns to optimise the customer experience. Maybe there is a rich history behind their unique products? I do not know the answer, but there was clearly a different culture at Agios Stefanos compared to the other five monasteries.

Why is it that one company manages to build a unique customer experience, while others fail miserably, even if the context and market conditions are identical? Could all the shops have been successful? Of course! What do they need to change and what steps would be involved? How does one polish a diamond in the rough?

Questions like these fascinate me! That's why I wrote this book.

IS YOUR BUSINESS A DIAMOND IN THE ROUGH?

Over the past 22 years, I have had the privilege of a front row seat, watching scores of companies as they succeeded or failed with customer-centric strategies, an approach that seems very simple on the surface, but is often difficult in practice. **Companies can easily become bogged down by rigid systems or faulty communication. A common complaint is, 'We have so much potential, but it remains untapped.'**

I have yet to meet a company that does not have good intentions for customer experience; (almost) everyone has the intention of getting it right. Yet, most companies remain diamonds in the rough in terms of customer experience: their customer experience potential is not fully exploited.

How can companies close this gap? How can their potential to create a winning customer experience be maximised? How does a company evolve from a diamond in the rough to a beautiful, sparkling and radiant diamond?

THAT IS WHAT THIS BOOK IS ABOUT, AND IT IS ONE I HAVE WANTED TO WRITE FOR A LONG TIME!

Some readers may be familiar with my previous books, such as, *The Offer You Can't Refuse*, a book about marketing strategy and vision. It, along with my other books, was based on theory and used market data to derive marketing models. *A Diamond in the Rough* is different. It is made up of stories and practical tips from my personal experience gained during more than two decades of consulting in the field, involving hundreds of company visits. Thus, this book is a compendium of practice-based market knowledge. I share my opinions and my insights. Do not expect great new theories, but rather lots of fresh insights and 'Aha!' moments to strengthen your customer-centricity in daily practice. Included are more than 100 concrete tips to improve your customer-centricity. The tips are woven into the text and summarised at the end of the book for your convenience.

Many of you already have your vision in focus but are still struggling with its execution. This book is designed to help you put your vision into practice.

This book is primarily a 'HOW?' book.
'HOW' can your company become more customer-centric? It would surely not be that difficult to make the other souvenir shops in Meteora work successfully. Yet it did not happen. What could the monks have done to change that? What role do managers play? How do managers build a culture where every employee is committed to work in a customer-focused manner every day?

I am very keen to help companies rapidly strengthen their customer focus, be they large or small companies, B2C or B2B, based in the East or the West. I am convinced that developing a radiant diamond mindset can make a difference in any type of company. My dream is to soon see numerous rough diamonds shining like beautiful jewels.

I suppose you are thinking, 'Actually, we are already one of those polished diamonds; is this book still for me?' I would like to invite you to read on, nonetheless. After all, shiny diamonds can become dusty and dull if they are not frequently polished. But above all: shiny diamond managers usually become excited by learning about customer-centricity. Shiny diamond managers are experts at picking up new ideas and adopting small changes that make the diamond shine just a little bit more. You are sure to find your fill of new and practical ideas in this book.

I wish you much inspiration and enjoyment reading this book, my sixth book on customer-centricity. As always, you can send your feedback directly to me. I love to read your stories and hear what aspects you have been working on. You can reach me via just about any social media or via my direct mail address: Steven@VanBelleghem.biz

THANKS FOR THE INSPIRATION, SIEBE

I owe the metaphor of the diamond to our eldest son, Siebe. He is passionate about science. One day he was studying different aspects of diamonds. When he told me about what he had learned, I was busy working on a new presentation for a client. His story about the evolution of diamonds immediately appealed to me. The following day, I used the metaphor of the rough diamond for the first time in a presentation. I noticed that it resonated with my audience, so I began using it. Eventually, it became the title of this new book.

Here, I will let Siebe explain in his own words how a diamond is formed. This scientific structure the evolution of a rough to a radiant diamond – is the basis for the structure of this book.

The next day I used the metaphor of *a diamond in the rough* for the first time in a presentation.

FROM A ROUGH DIAMOND TO A FINISHED GEM - THE SCIENTIFIC VERSION

By Siebe Van Belleghem, science enthusiast, 03-08-2009.

#1 WHAT IS A DIAMOND?

A diamond is, simply explained, a mineral that crystallises under immense pressure after a long time and eventually becomes a rough diamond under the influence of pure carbon. To make this possible, you need a few crucial elements. Enormous pressure, pure carbon and a matrix. A matrix is the 'mother' of the diamond. It is the stone in which the diamond is formed. A matrix can consist of materials other than ordinary stone, for example: copper ore, iron ore and sometimes gold.

The matrix can affect the diamond's appearance by increasing the concentration of magnesium, for example. This can cause the diamond to look different in colour: pink, black, green or red are colours you wouldn't expect to see on a diamond. This is probably because bright diamonds are most often used on jewellery such as rings. According to many, this is also the most beautiful colour for a diamond.

Coloured diamonds are often mistaken for other valuable minerals like rubies, emeralds and topazes because of the colour. No matter how similar other gemstones are to diamonds, the difference lies in the hardness. Diamonds are the hardest material in the world, making them the only ones to achieve a perfect 10 on the Mohs hardness scale. Any gemstone that does not reach a score of 10 is therefore not a diamond.

Before diamonds are treated, they are rough diamonds. Rough diamonds have a rough surface and usually have irregular shapes. When a diamond is made in a lab, they use a method called crystallisation. This makes them look more like an eight-sided die. A useful tip to tell the difference between a natural diamond and a lab-made diamond is to use a magnifying glass to look for a series of numbers on the diamond. If you see those, then it is lab-made; if not then you have a natural diamond. Obviously, the lab-made diamond is worth less because it is less rare, but that does not mean it is less beautiful. Most people will never see the difference.

#2 FROM ROUGH DIAMOND TO BRIGHT DIAMOND

A lot of steps are required to turn a rough diamond into a diamond worthy of a ring. Let's start with the most important steps that will drastically change the look.

Rough diamonds always have a lot of internal cracks that don't look pretty. Those cracks are removed with a special oil applied to cover the culprits. They will still be there; you just will not see them anymore. A rough diamond also often has discolourations caused by internal dust, which causes the diamond to look a bit cloudy instead of bright. To ensure that those discolourations do not lower the quality, they are burned away by heat treatment.

To make the rough surface nice and smooth, we need harder means (literally). **To sand a diamond, you need diamond-lined tools, because only a material that is at least as hard can make a diamond nice and smooth. This is how you get a bright diamond.** Then, despite all these procedures, it still doesn't look like a diamond you would see on a ring. It looks more like a glass cone with a cut edge.

#3 FROM BRIGHT DIAMOND TO FINISHED GEM

Next, the diamond is cut. This is done using special tools, usually made from artificial substances that are at least as hard. **The diamond is cut in such a special way that most of the light entering the diamond frontally is reflected out through the many facets at the bottom.** This creates a stunning effect called 'fire' because of its reddish colour.

The diamond is now ready for the final step. The diamond is very carefully placed on the ring. To ensure that the diamond does not fall off the ring, it is held by four or sometimes three prongs. These arms are then bent to fully secure the diamond. That was the final step; the diamond ring is ready to be sold.

CHAPTER 1

A DIAMOND IN THE ROUGH

'WHEN YOU TRY YOUR BEST **BUT** *YOU DON'T SUCCEED'*

COLDPLAY - FIX YOU

A POLISHED DIAMOND IN THE CONSTRUCTION SECTOR

If there is one sector where there is still room to grow in terms of customer focus, it is the construction sector. I do not know what your experience is with construction companies, but mine is not terribly positive. How often are appointments to build or repair something cancelled at the last minute? How often are the agreed budgets overspent? Confidence in pricing is so low that people automatically assume they will pay 30% more than the quoted price. And if the final budget does not exceed that 30% buffer, customers are satisfied. There are truly a lot of diamonds in the rough in this sector.

The exception that proves the rule: I recently had the opportunity to give a presentation for the construction company ibens and was impressed by their customer experience. Martin Geernaart, one of ibens' co-CEOs, asked me, 'What do construction companies always have problems with?' The answer was simple: respecting the agreed budget (friction 1), meeting the agreed timing (friction 2), combined with poor communication with the customer (friction 3).

These three frictions are where ibens excels. Their mission statement reads as follows: realise clients' building dreams within their available resources. Their success formula is to have the architects and engineers work with the team that maintains the client relationship. If architects are given free rein on a project, they tend to overdesign, and engineers are inclined to propose the latest technology. This translates into overspend. If all parties collaborate from the start, this source of customer friction is addressed from the outset and a 'bickering culture' is avoided. When the plan and budget are mutually agreed upon, it is difficult to assign blame to another party if something goes wrong. Consequently, the team tends to devise solutions that keep projects on track.

The managers at ibens prefer to have long-term contracts with their partners and they make a point of paying them correctly and on time. If something goes wrong in a project resulting in a cost overrun, ibens absorbs it. Without discussion! The job security offered to partners, combined with prompt payment, translates into risk containment. This results in strong bonds between ibens and their construction partners and motivates them to adhere to project schedules. This philosophy eliminates the second friction (timing).

People from the construction industry can make a very strong counter argument: that given the price inflation of building materials and logistics challenges in recent years, these things are beyond their control.

But ibens also faces these difficulties. This is when the art of communication comes in. For example, if there are difficulties with supplies from China, for example, a conversation with the customer starts immediately. *'Look, dear customer, we have a problem. The product you have chosen is currently unavailable, but here is a similar product that we can deliver to you at short notice. You can choose to stay with your first choice, but if you do, we expect delivery to be delayed by four weeks.'* This is an example of how to offer customers a choice and a solution by being proactive and transparent, two aspects of communication that customers love.

The team at ibens offers a very clear promise to customers in their mission statement. This mission is clear internally and externally. It reflects empathy and partnership radiating like a diamond between ibens, its partners and its customers. This book profiles companies that succeed in taking their customer experience to the next level, that are radiant like diamonds. **The approach at ibens can be implemented anywhere and in any type of market.** Unfortunately, most companies today are rough rather than polished diamonds.

HOW DISNEY MESSED UP A MARRIAGE PROPOSAL

We are all very big Disney fans in our family, including the movies and the theme parks. Recently, we revisited Disney World in Florida. We really enjoyed the atmosphere there, the beautiful decorations and the high quality of the attractions. As a customer experience enthusiast, I also appreciate their efficiency and the friendliness and flexibility of the staff. Every detail of the customer experience has been well thought out and their employees demonstrate pride in working for Disney. This combination is worth its weight in gold.

Despite Disney's impressive track record in customer experience, things do go wrong from time to time. In mid-2021, a young man planned a momentous event at Disney. He wanted to ask his girlfriend to marry him at Disneyland Paris. They arrived at Sleeping Beauty's castle at midday where he invited her to stand on a small stage in front of the castle. When he dropped to his knees, the young woman immediately knew what was going on. She clasped her hands in front of her mouth when he showed her the the ring and asked 'the' question. His friends were filming everything, and passers-by looked on with delight as this beautiful moment unfolded. Suddenly, a Disney employee wearing a Mickey Mouse hat stormed onto the stage, leaned over and snatched the ring out of the young man's hands before the girl had a chance to reply. The employee pompously directed the couple to continue to a spot next to the stage. Goodbye atmosphere! Goodbye romance! Goodbye unique video to show the kids later!

Why did this go so wrong?

One of Disney's strengths is their extremely solid processes and procedures. These are designed to facilitate the circulation of large groups of people through a busy theme park in comfort and to ensure the safety of customers and employees. During this marriage proposal, Disney's strength became a weakness. The employee in question followed the process perfectly: guests are not allowed on stage. In this case, the employee did not sense that this was a unique moment. Perhaps this situation could have been handled differently? The staff member had good intentions and followed the rules, but the execution was not ideal. Even beautiful diamonds sometimes have their rough edges.

THE SLIDE IN EVERYONE'S PRESENTATION

Do you have it too? The PowerPoint slide in your presentation where customer focus is described as one of your objectives? This theme has, no doubt, been presented several times to your employees as well. This is a good intention, but one that does not often go beyond the slide. Companies can convince themselves that they offer excellent customer service and be quite shocked at customer research that demonstrates that this is not the case. A statistic that has become a classic in the world of customer-centricity is: **80% of CEOs think their company is customer-centric, but only 8% of customers agree**[1]. There is a huge gap between what companies think they achieve and how effectively it comes across to customers.

There can even be a big difference in perception between a company's management and employees. I chatted briefly with the CEO of a large e-commerce company to fine-tune a presentation I was about to make at one of their events. 'Steven,' he said, 'in terms of customer experience, we are doing very well.' As I prepared my computer for the presentation, the IT team came by to help me with the technology. A member of the team asked, *'What is the topic of your presentation?'*
'Customer focus,' I replied.

'That's very good; we still have a lot to learn about customer focus. It goes completely haywire here so often.'

A DIAMOND IN THE ROUGH

Do you recognise this paradox? Your company has the will to become customer-centric. Your company has made plans to become customer-centric, yet your company fails to excel in customer-centricity.

This problem is the great paradox in the world of customer-centricity: just about every company has good intentions, but most of the time the execution is only average in quality.

Of course, there are different levels of customer-centric intention and execution:

- ◆ Graphite. Presumably they exist, but I have only rarely encountered them, that is, organisations that have no intention of building a good relationship with the public. Their chances of success at becoming customer-centric are virtually non-existent, of course. The only organisations that would be classified here are phishing organisations. Their aim is to rob the public. They are the opposite of customer-centric, yet unfortunately they often succeed.
- ◆ Fake Diamonds. Occasionally, I come across organisations that have good stories about their customer experience, but which I find are substandard in practice.
- ◆ Rough Diamonds. These are companies that yearn to be very customer-centric, but cannot get past certain barriers, meaning that they never get complimentary feedback and so they lose motivation and remain stuck in the middle ground. This is where most companies are found. These organisations are not bad at customer-centricity, but they do not excel at it either.
- ◆ Frustrated Rough Diamonds. I always feel sorry for the employees of these companies. Everyone wants so badly to excel in customer focus. Their intentions are higher than average, but their execution is mediocre. Often these companies are bumping up against far too complex internal structures which hamper flexibility of execution that is required to really excel.
- ◆ The Polished Diamond! The dream! These are the companies that know very well how they are going to make the customer happy and manage to make it happen.

In the remainder of this book, I want to take you on that adventure: to hone the rough diamonds into a beautiful, bright and polished diamonds. But first, let us review when and how this adventure has gone wrong for so many companies, beginning in the 1980s.

CREATION OF ROUGH DIAMONDS IN THE 1980S

The shareholder value model became popular in the 1980s. The term, shareholder value model, was first mentioned in *Fortune* magazine in 1962. Eight years later, economist Milton Friedman introduced his 'Friedman doctrine' in an essay for *The New York Times*. His main point was that a company has no responsibility to society or the general public; its only responsibility is to its shareholders. About 10 years later GE's CEO, Jack Welch, gave a speech entitled *Growing Fast in a Slow-Growth Economy*, widely seen as the beginning of the obsession with the *shareholder value model*. Since then, this theory has guided a lot of leaders and investors.

The ultimate objective of the shareholder value model is a rising share price. As a result, decisions are not made for the long-term good of the company, but rather for the short-term impact on the share price. A company that fires employees to cut costs is often rewarded by the stock market with a rising share price. A company that announces that it will invest more in R&D and innovation to create long-term value often gets punished by the stock market. This is how the market works. For instance, numerous analysts criticised Meta's (rebranded Facebook) massive investment in the Metaverse. Zuckerberg's company was punished on the stock market because of its hefty R&D costs until he began to reduce expenses by firing people and the stock rose again. And the crazy thing is that everyone thinks this is logical. After all, investing too much in *the day after tomorrow* is bad for short-term shareholder value.

Another trend that began in the 1980s was the creation of private equity funds that piled into technology companies and pressured management for rapid ramp-ups in value. Forty years later, the world still operates according to this model, one which does not always benefit the customer experience. Rough diamonds that are managed in this way tend to remain rough diamonds because they are often compelled to target short-term financial results at the cost of building long-term customer trust.

Fortunately, a big change in terms of social interest is now emerging. The Friedman doctrine, where the sole focus is financial profit, is thankfully no longer considered as the preferred template for corporate strategy. However, the workings of the financial markets continue to ensure that companies remain focused on the short term. Higher prices, indexation of wages and general market pressures force many organisations into cost-cutting mode. This is understandable, of course, but if this reduces the quality of service, it degrades long-term customer relationships. Many readers will have felt this dichotomy: you want to do something for customers, but the pressure on short-term financial results is sometimes so great that the customer comes second. The enormous pressure on short-term financial results is the biggest cause of average customer service (diamonds in the rough). A long-term mindset will be one of the necessary elements for companies to evolve from rough to polished diamonds.

TECHNOLOGY IS NOT A SHORT CUT TO ENHANCED CUSTOMER EXPERIENCE

The Peter Principle was described by Dr Laurence J. Peter in his 1969 book, *The Peter Principle: Why things always go wrong*. The Peter Principle is the observation that in a fixed hierarchy, people are promoted until they reach their level of incompetence. In other words, people are promoted based on success in their existing role into a new role for which they may not have sufficient competences. I believe the Peter Principle can be applied to many technologies. For example, many people (I plead guilty in part) believed that technology would offer short cuts to higher customer satisfaction. 'If we buy technology X or Y, satisfaction will increase.' But the promise of some new technologies has been over-estimated. They have been promoted for uses that are beyond their capacity.

Artificial intelligence, augmented and virtual reality (metaverse), crypto, NFT, Web3, Blockchain and other technologies have unique applications and strong stories that excite many people. Many of them have been promoted as having a high potential to also improve the customer experience, but their success rates are low. Investing in technology is a necessity, but this alone will not transform companies into polished diamonds: there is no short cut to a great customer experience.

Of the various technologies that have emerged over the past decade, only mobile technology and e-commerce have demonstrated success in improving the customer experience. Indeed, technology devoid of a mobile component now seems unthinkable. Mobile technology has clear benefits that enhance the quality of the customer experience. It increases service speed, enables high quality self-service and permits personalisation and new communication options. All these benefits have become standard features of the company/

customer interface. The same applies to e-commerce. The ability to find almost any product online and to receive it at home the next day has increased convenience for many consumers. The amount of time an average family can save thanks to e-commerce is incredible.

Many other technologies can be described by the Peter Principle. Consider the role of voice assistants, for example. In my 2017 book, *Customers the Day After Tomorrow*, I wrote enthusiastically about their potential. By 2018, this technology was working at 80% of its theoretical potential, allowing me to envision various customer experience possibilities. Who does not dream of a personal assistant who can book appointments and proactively arrange all kinds of things? Or imagine being able to automatically order products through a digital butler. As I write this book in 2023, this technology has achieved only 10% more of its potential. It has not yet delivered on its promise.

The same can be said about self-driving cars. In 2014, I was convinced that our eldest son Siebe would no longer need a driving licence. The car would pick him up and bring him back later. Now we are nine years on (Siebe is 14) and it is 100% certain that he will have to drive the car himself when he reaches driving age. The concept of self-driving cars still captures my imagination, but until the technology achieves a 100% safety level, the transition will not happen. For example, if planes could only make a successful landing 99% of the time, there would be about 1,000 plane crashes a day.

Customer service chatbots are another underperformer, frustrating more people than they help. In theory, chatbots seem great: machines respond to routine customer inquiries, while humans respond to more complex, emotional questions. I am a huge proponent of this principle, but in practice, most chatbots fail at answering even the simplest questions. Forty-six percent of consumers become frustrated when they cannot choose a human at the start of a customer service query[2] and 55% say it takes too many questions before a chatbot realises that it does not know the answer to the question or does not even understand the question[3].

In short, we expect too much from technology too soon, making it incompetent for the task at hand. Another demonstration that there is no short cut for improving the company-client relationship.

WHAT IF TECHNOLOGY REACHES THE 99% STANDARD?

In late 2022, the world got to know ChatGPT – an AI chatbot developed by Open AI. The enthusiasm was enormous. In just two months, the platform had more than 100 million active users. That makes ChatGPT the fastest adopted software tool ever in history[4]. In comparison, TikTok took nine months to reach 100 million users and Instagram 30 months. The reason for the enthusiasm is easy to explain: ChatGPT produces useful output in seconds.

Have you also had the ChatGPT conversation with your children? How are we going to use this technology for school? Will your kids be allowed to use it? For which tasks will its use be permitted and for which tasks not? Does your school have a policy on this? At some point during 2023, most students probably submitted a task created with this AI homework assistant, only to wait anxiously to see if the teacher caught on. I think we are all secretly jealous. If only we had such a tool during our student days, right?

Was there a ChatGPT conversation during Q1 2023 in your company too? Were there discussions about which tasks to use it for and how to apply it? For example, junior copywriters questioned the survival of their jobs as the AI content output is at least as good as what some entry-level copywriters produce. ChatGPT will not replace top journalism, but it could very well replace authors with average writing ability.

The potential of ChatGPT has revived enthusiasm for artificial intelligence because it offers tangible proof of AI's potential and, thus, provides added value. It excels at the job it was designed for, so it does not fit the Peter Principle. It is generally accepted that ChatGPT still sometimes generates errors, yet these are seen as acceptable shortcomings in view of its potential. So, the question arises: can this kind of technology take the customer experience to the next level once it becomes 99% error free? The answer is clear: of course. Just as the smartphone has brought new experiences and possibilities, artificial intelligence will undoubtedly do the same.

Artificial intelligence will increase personalisation, make communication between internal and external people more efficient and in doing so open the door to more proactive services. These are all elements that customers value. However, new technologies require ongoing investment to succeed in meeting the requirements of the modern customer.

Can this high-performance form of AI (or some other new breakthrough technology) be enough to transform your business from a rough to a polished diamond?

CUSTOMER CULTURE IS THE BASIS FOR POLISHED DIAMONDS

Rien Brus, a customer experience (CX) consultant responsible for customer-driven transformation at pension administrator APG, made the following important point during a recent conversation: *'Every time I see a new technology, I can be so impressed by it. After a few months, there is no longer astonishment, it has become a normal part of life. Sometimes I even expect more from it and those expectations are not met. However, when I meet a company with a genuine customer culture where you feel how people are genuinely interested in their customers, well, that never becomes normal. That never gets boring. That continues to make me feel good every time.'*

The business community focused too much on short-term financial results during the 1980s. In the first 20 years of the new millennium, we were overly optimistic about the potential for new technology to enhance customer satisfaction. Despite the benefits of new technologies, they are not enough to make a sustainable difference in customer satisfaction. After all, ChatGPT is available for every company in the world. Initially one company may be able to use the technology more effectively than another, but this is advantage will erode very quickly. The technology will become necessary for success but like most technologies, it will very quickly become a minimum requirement and not a sustainable differentiator for success.

It is becoming increasingly clear that the only sustainable way to make customers truly satisfied is by creating a culture where the customer is truly at the centre. This is an environment where both the leaders and employees of an organisation are imbued with customer-centricity. This is a culture where everyone realises that a satisfied customer is the guarantee of future success. It is a culture that is willing to suffer short-term pain to ensure long-term success. And do not get me wrong: being profitable and achieving solid financial results are obviously part of that. It is necessary to be able to make customers happy and continue to invest in your customer experience. Pieter Zwart, founder and CEO of Dutch e-commerce company Coolblue, expresses it well: 'When I started Coolblue, I had two goals. I very much wanted to become a multimillionaire and I very much wanted to have the most satisfied customers. That's why the finance director and customer satisfaction director are the two most important people in the company. Meanwhile, I can say that both objectives have been achieved.'

To become a polished diamond, it is necessary to see customer focus as an ongoing, long-term philosophy of your company. In the first few months after the COVID pandemic, it became very painfully clear that customer experience does not work like a Christmas tree. You cannot just turn your customer-centricity on and off when it suits you.  Thirty-two percent of consumers feel that customer service is lower after the pandemic than before[5]. Forty percent of US consumers sense a drop in productivity and responsiveness of contact centres compared to the period before the pandemic[6].

The chaos at European airports during the summer of 2022 was the ultimate proof. The airline industry had put its customer experience on hold for almost two years. Travel restarted very rapidly after the corona crisis, but the industry failed to restart its focus on customer experience with equal speed. Again, managing the customer experience is not like throwing lights on a Christmas tree and switching them on and off when it suits you. It requires a stable vision and excellent execution.

A strong customer culture leads to a spiral of positive effects:

1. *A strong customer experience*. If a company has a strong customer culture, employees are trained to put the customer first. Moreover, they have the freedom to decide what is best for each specific customer. As a result, the customer gets a strong and personalised experience.

2. *Higher customer loyalty*. A better customer experience leads to higher customer loyalty. Eighty-three percent of customers say they change suppliers because of poor customer service[7], and more than half of customers are even willing to pay more for a company with excellent service[8].

3. *A positive reputation*. A strong customer culture leads to a stronger brand reputation, as customers are more likely to talk positively about a customer-centric company.

4. *Competitive advantage*. Customers today have more choice than ever. Moreover, the barrier to switching suppliers is lower than ever. A strong customer experience and good reputation make customers more likely to buy your products and services, leading to better financial results.

The faster this customer culture spirals within your organisation, the faster you can overtake competitors.

In a recent study by Salesforce, one of the key conclusions was that 88% of people value the product as much as the experience[9]. The well-known marketing strategist, Seth Godin, jokingly commented on this study saying, *'Perhaps those other 12% didn't understand the question properly.'* Of course, a good product is essential, but the importance of customer experience in making a purchase can be variable; but it is on the rise as Enrico Ceriani, AGC Glass Europe VP, pointed out in a recent presentation: *'Our products and even our innovation will not differentiate us in the coming years. When we innovate, it usually provides a temporary advantage. The competition has become very good at copying our innovations quickly. The only thing that can give us a long-term competitive advantage is our customer culture. Our customer culture will ensure that we remain profitable in the long run.'*

A strong customer culture is the key to transforming your organisation from a diamond in the rough to a polished diamond. It is this aspect of a company's strength that is the hardest to copy.

FROM A DIAMOND IN THE ROUGH TO A POLISHED DIAMOND

In this book I describe how to transform a diamond in the rough (average customer culture) into a polished diamond (customer culture is a sustainable differentiator of your business). The book is organised in three parts.

PART 1: THE BRIGHT DIAMOND

The first transformative step to turn a rough diamond into a beautiful jewel is to clarify the route towards perfection. Clarity of vision: that is what both employees and customers need. **Leaders do not need to convince people that their vision is correct.** Leaders must bring employees to a shared conviction that a customer-centric vision is right for the company. What small decisions are needed to encourage belief in your vision? The more people there are who believe that you are committed to your vision, the more clarity you can provide and the brighter the diamond will become (Chapter 4).

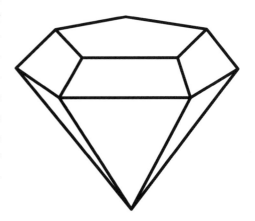

Moreover, in this gloomy world, it is necessary for leaders to radiate a good number of positive vibes (Chapter 2). Most people are tired of negative newsflow and consciously seek positive messages. Positivity builds enthusiasm amongst people and can act as a magnet to unify them.

Additionally, customers expect leaders to provide clarity about their company's social conscience and influence (Chapter 3). How will companies use their influence to create added social value? The public increasingly expects companies to take responsibility for influencing a range of social issues, in addition to the climate challenge. This extends to making a difference to people in need in the local community.

PART 2: THE CUT DIAMOND

In the second part, we facet the bright diamond into a beautiful jewel. A company with a true customer culture looks at customer loyalty in a different way than a rough diamond company does. Rough diamonds expect customer loyalty to start with the customer; customers are rewarded once their loyalty is proven. Bright diamonds look at the company/customer relationship from the opposite perspective: customer loyalty starts with the company and as a result the customer rewards the company with their loyalty (Chapter 5).

A key component of strong customer loyalty is empathy. But empathy is a rather vague concept, one that is rarely addressed in a business context. I believe in organised empathy where empathy is structurally integrated into the business processes (Chapter 6).

A last step in the fashioning of a gemstone is to cut it into the best shape for the given stone, using the right technology in the right way (Chapter 7). Rough diamond companies often use technology too early in the process, hoping to quickly resolve problems with their customer experience. In contrast, clear and bright diamonds use technology to optimise the performance of their teams or to provide greater customer efficiency or relevance. Clear and bright diamonds do not get excited by the technology, but rather by the customer benefits that it provides.

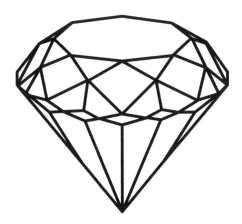

PART 3: CUSTOMER FOCUS IN 'THE NEVER NORMAL'

The world and therefore the context of the customer is in a constant state of change. Over the past 20 years, we have weathered one major societal shock after another. Moreover, it seems as if the social shocks are arriving ever more quickly. The worldwide havoc caused by COVID was not yet fully digested when Putin invaded Ukraine causing an energy and inflation crisis. Meanwhile, we are all aware of seasonal disruptions to the climate. **After COVID, many people talked about the emergence of a *'new normal'*. There was hope that this new normal would usher in a stable period. Nothing could be further from the truth. There is no *new normal*.** In the last part of this book, I will zoom in on customer-centric entrepreneurship in what my friend and business partner Peter Hinssen calls 'the never normal'. Currently, there are so many challenges (climate, war, inflation, refugees, the Chinese Super League ...) that it is a certainty that doing business will not get any easier in the coming years. Entrepreneurs in this never normal (Chapter 8, written by Peter Hinssen) also must deal with a never normal customer (Chapter 9). Customers' expectations of companies are not only increasing, they are also fundamentally shifting. In the final pages of the book, I discuss in detail how customer-centricity is evolving into the never normal. After all, if this is the new normal then this is the context in which the transformation from rough to polished diamond must take place. It is important to understand this context to be able to respond to it wisely later.

THE BRIGHT DIAMOND

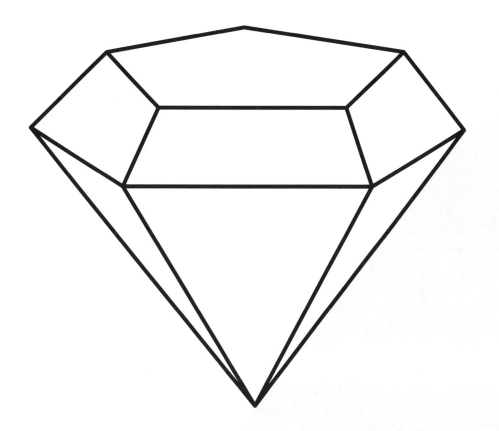

PART 1: THE BRIGHT DIAMOND

Rough diamonds do not live up to their customer experience ambitions. They get stuck in mediocrity. How do you manage to turn that rough diamond into a beautiful, shining diamond? That transformation happens in two steps. **This part of the book details the first step: the rough diamond becomes a bright diamond.**

Before you can start cutting you need that bright diamond, which can only develop with leadership and clarity of vision. Every involved stakeholder, and that includes employees, man-agement and external partners, needs to know what your company stands for. Immediately one thinks of formu-lating a mission statement or a Simon Sinek-style 'Why' statement. But that is not my intent. In fact, you probably already have a mission statement or know what it says.

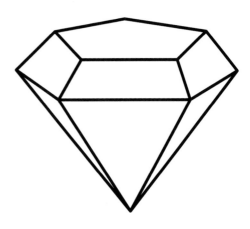

This is a book about building customer cultures. How do you get your employ-ees excited about helping customers in the best way possible? How can you get customers excited about your company? That is the goal of my book. The first step in building a customer culture is to provide clarity by ensuring that all stakeholders have a clear understanding of your ambitions. Clarity provides a foundation that you can build on. Part 1 describes the different components you need to make it very clear to all stakeholders that you genuinely want to build a customer culture.

What vibe does your company exude? (Chapter 2: The TOP GUN Effect)
Is your profile in the market positive or negative? When you are interviewed by the media, do you complain or do you announce an innovation? Some compa-nies are portrayed by the media as complainers. This is a missed opportunity. A bright diamond has a positive media profile. If you want people to become

enthusiastic about your company you must first and foremost exude enthusiasm and positivity.

What social influence does your company have? (Chapter 3: The Circle of Influence)
In the past, companies were mainly concerned with their own problems. In some cases, a company may have acted to help their industry, but that was all. Today, companies influence all social issues. How far does your influence extend? And how do you use that influence to make a positive contribution?

What credibility does your message have with your employees? (Chapter 4: The Belief)
One of the biggest problems in achieving a truly customer-centric company is internal credibility. In many companies, employees do not believe management. A lot has to do with the micro communication and decisions of the leaders. Employees look at leaders' behaviour much more than they value their words. Do your employees believe your ambitions in terms of customer focus?

CHAPTER 2

THE TOP GUN EFFECT

'OPTIMISM IS A **MORAL DUTY'**

KARL POPPER

PEOPLE LONG FOR BLUE, SUNNY SKIES

When Europe's energy crisis reached its peak in the summer of 2022, the media made a hobby of looking for people who could no longer pay their bills. Bakers and butchers recounted how their bills had tripled, making it unprofitable to continue working. Day after day, people were made to face up to how bleak the future would be. Belgian Prime Minister Alexander De Croo put it very harshly at one point: 'The next five to 10 winters will be difficult.' Moreover, these people had to digest these gloomy messages only three months after the COVID restrictions began to be relaxed and they had begun to hope that life might return to normal.

Bleak times can cause people to become reflective and to wonder what it is, exactly, that they are longing for. The answer is simple. Imagine that the sky is brooding and grey for days on end, it is pouring with rain, the wind is howling, so, what do you long for? Right! A bright, blue sky.

As an analogy, customers do not want to listen to their supplier grumbling about their problems. Steve Jobs put it perfectly: **'Your customers don't care about you. They don't care about your product or service. They care about themselves, their dreams, their goals.** Now, they will care much more if you help them reach their goals, and to do that, you must understand their goals, as well as their needs and deepest desires.'

This is not to suggest that customers are not sorry that their baker's energy prices are rising. But the reason they are sorry is mainly because they are afraid prices will rise yet again for them as well. When you are dining in a restaurant, you do not want to listen to the chef complaining that it is hard to find good staff. You are there to enjoy good food and have a good time. You need to listen to the chef's complaints just as much as you need a sore thumb. Customers are mainly interested in their own challenges. A company's job is to help the customer with those challenges and provide value.

This does not mean that you should never utter a negative comment to your customers. If a problem arises you need to discuss it with the customer to protect your relationship with them. But the problem should not be the focus of your communication. In the example of the restaurant, when a customer specifically asks about an issue, the restaurateur should respond in a way that demonstrates a benefit for the customer. 'It is indeed difficult to find staff, but we are now working on a new technology that will increase our efficiency, so you as a customer will not be affected. Quite the contrary!' Messages like this are exactly what customers are looking for. A fun and worthwhile exercise is to think of some difficulties you might have that customers could become aware of and formulate positive responses. By thinking about potential problems and practising dialogues in advance, you will be ready when the question comes your way.

The choice is simple. Rather than howling with the wolves, let us consciously ensure positive communication with our customers. In the current social and financial environment, we need positivity and a positive impact for our businesses more than ever.

THE TOP GUN EFFECT

I became more convinced than ever of the power of positivity during the summer of 2022 on the day our family went to the cinema to enjoy *Top Gun Maverick*. I must admit that the four of us are big fans of Tom Cruise and the Top Gun films. We had been looking forward to going to the film for months. We enjoyed it so much that a few weeks later we returned to the cinema to relive the film a second time.

For those who have not yet seen *Top Gun Maverick*, take note: there are some spoilers coming up. The great thing about the film is the pure feel-good-vibe that the film exudes. From the moment you hear the soundtrack and moments later you watch Tom Cruise pull off his leather jacket and cruise off on his motorbike, you know the film will be great. The crazy thing is that although the film is set in a military context and a US Air Force fighter jet is on screen throughout almost the entire film, no one dies in the film and there are no bad guys. The story is totally predictable: at the beginning, Tom Cruise is presented with a kind of 'Mission Impossible' (of course). But you know he will succeed! The mission is a success and Tom is the big hero. You expect this outcome, yet the film is exciting.

The question is: are people looking for this at present: feel-good stories with predictable endings and simple scenarios devoid of the complexity of some of the Netflix series? And the answer is, emphatically: YES! *Top Gun Maverick* was the best reviewed[10] and highest grossing[11] film of 2022. This is positivity with impact. My invitation: add some Top Gun Effect to your customer experience. Maintain a positive mindset and strive to give your customers that feel-good factor.

THE TOP GUN EFFECT IN PRACTICE

A rewarding exercise is to think of ways that your organisation can add the Top Gun Effect to your customer experience. How can this effect be used to improve the feel-good factor of your collaboration with customers? How can you radiate that positivity? The Top Gun Effect is often found in small things. The Magic Castle Hotel[12] in Los Angeles is a very simple and somewhat strange looking hotel. It is painted pink and has castle-like features here and there. The rooms are nothing special and the pool is very small. Yet it is the tenth best-rated hotel in Los Angeles on Trip Advisor. Most reviewers rate the hotel highly because of 'The Popsicle Hotline', a red telephone by the pool. Twenty-four hours a day, you can lift the handset and order free ice cream. I do not need to tell you how crazy children are about that phone.

Other examples are the initiatives of JetBlue's CEO. Everyone knows how annoying it can be to wait around in an airport. But JetBlue passengers are sometimes surprised by occasional visits from the CEO who hands out drinks and donuts to his customers while they wait to board. Sometimes there are surprises on the flights: one example was a quiz. The winner received a free JetBlue flight. In response to a major delay of one of their flights, all affected passengers were given free flights. **Positive vibes and surprises. What little surprises can you use to make your customers feel positive?**

Louis Vuitton sent a message of positivity to customers using visual communication at their shops undergoing complete makeovers in the beginning of January 2023. Yayoi Kusama decorated the facade and interior of their New York City shop with her famous sparkly polka dots. A Louis Vuitton shop in Paris received a robot version of Kusama painting yellow dots on its windows. A giant puppet of her appearing to be painting its facade adorns their Champs-Élysées shop. In this way, the shops all radiate cheerfulness. To top it off, a Snapchat filter has been created that enables users to make coloured polka dots appear on any historic building, a simple means to bring joy to customers. It is time to unleash the Top Gun Effect on your customers.

THE TOP GUN EFFECT ON SOCIAL MEDIA: GAS

Why are TikTok and Snapchat so popular? Because they are more positive and entertaining than other social networks. Anyone who has ever sat with their kids playing with the many Snapchat filters knows perfectly well what I mean. Or perhaps you have already collaborated with your kids on some (supposedly) funny TikTok videos. Making TikTok videos has become somewhat of a shared pastime in many families. The takehome message is that the objective of creating videos is no longer about the number of views or likes, but mainly about having fun while making the video.

Fun and positive social media are on the rise. The new GAS social network, for instance, is enjoying tremendous growth. It launched in August 2022 and by October 2022 had more than 500,000 users.[13] The name GAS comes from the phrase 'gassing someone up' which translates as 'boosting their self-confidence'. The concept is very simple: the app invites teenagers to complement each other. The founder of GAS is Nikita Bier who is also the founder of a forerunner app with a similar mission, tbh or 'to be honest'. Facebook bought tbh in 2017 but did nothing with it and the concept died a quiet death. 'The reason I built it [GAS] was because I wanted to bring back what tbh did for so many kids five years ago, which was raise self-esteem and spread positivity,' says Bier.[14]

THE SCIENCE BEHIND THE TOP GUN EFFECT

Tom Cruise's character does not doubt for a second that he will make the mission a success. He is confident in his abilities and believes his instincts combined with his experience will make a difference. His hopes are based on reality. He is optimistic about his chances of success without being blind to the dangers of the mission. His positivity ultimately proves to be a driver of his team's success.

My belief in the Top Gun Effect is not just based on my gut feeling after seeing *Top Gun Maverick*. It is underpinned by science (though it is referred to by scientists as the science of optimism instead of the Top Gun Effect).

Tom's character says, 'In uncertain times, I always expect a positive outcome.' He could have said, 'If something can go wrong for me, it definitely will.'

Which outlook is closest to yours? Your choice can reveal a lot about how your life is currently going. Researchers studying optimism have found that your outlook can have major consequences for your wellbeing and your future[15]. People who tend to be optimistic and identify with the first sentence, tend to be healthier, feel mentally stronger and are often more successful than more pessimistic people who identify with the second sentence.

Optimistic people expect positive things to happen in their lives. Optimism does not mean completely denying negative things or certain risks. It is all about mindset. Even if there are challenges and difficulties, optimists continue to believe that things will turn out well for them. I am very grateful that I identify 100% with the first sentence. I have faith that things will turn out well and that most people around me have positive intentions. Sometimes I meet people who have 'problems' like mine. They see them as big pits in the road, while for me they seem like small wrinkles. I view problems as part of life, while they dwell on them for days. If you are surrounded by negative or pessimistic people, you may be surprised by how much of your energy is destroyed by their negativity, when it would be more impactful (and fun) to use that energy for more positive things. Ultimately, everyone has limited energy; it is best to spend it on positive things.

Optimism correlates with better mental health. Optimistic students are less stressed by exams than negative students. Optimistic mothers experience less postnatal depression than do negative mothers. Moreover, optimistic people in general suffer less from depression than negative people.[16]

Optimism also makes people more successful. A Forbes study demonstrated that optimistic employees are 103% more motivated to perform in their jobs.[17] Optimistic employees not only make themselves feel better, they also create a better atmosphere and dynamic that improves the performance of entire teams. An optimistic leader conveys good vibes to their team and builds self-confidence; a pessimistic leader puts a damper on enthusiasm and confidence.

The positivity of optimistic people is something other people love. Positive energy is almost like feeling the warmth of the sun. It brightens people up. It is more fun working with positive people. If you manage to radiate that positive atmosphere as a company, you become more successful almost automatically. It works like a magnet. If you want to recruit customer-oriented employees, you could almost conclude that one characteristic is enough: is this person rather optimistic or rather pessimistic? Choose optimistic employees to add the Top Gun Effect to your customer relationships; the job skills can be learned.

THE RISK OF NEGATIVE BIAS

Why is it so difficult for many organisations to stay committed to the Top Gun Effect? Staying positive is not easy for everyone. Many people suffer from what is known as the negativity bias.[18] The pilots on Tom Cruise's team in *Top Gun Maverick* failed time and again on the 'Mission Impossible' project. As time went on this weighed on the team and they began to focus only on the negative.

I have long used the Disney film *Inside Out* in my presentations to illustrate the principle of negative bias. The film tells the story of a teenage girl who changes schools. The story is told through the perspective of the girl's emotions. The viewer learns that there are five basic emotions: joy, sadness, envy, fear and anger. Four of the five emotions are negatively charged. No wonder we complain and whine so much. We cannot help it; we are programmed to complain. The same phenomena happens in our relationships with customers. If five out of 100 customers respond in a mean and arrogant way to staff, statistically that is a very small group of problem cases. In practice, however, we give so much weight to this group that after a while that five percent can seem to be the average customer. In my previous book, *The Offer You Can't Refuse*, I referred to this phenomenon, the negative bias, as the 95/5% rule in customer experience. The danger of the negative bias is that after a while you start tailoring procedures for the five percent, which in a way punishes the 95%. That is the most dangerous risk of being influenced by the negative bias.

Dr Jane McGonigal's 'urgent optimism' model works well to counter negative bias. McGonigal is a game designer whose research aims to translate the positive effects of gaming into concrete advice for individuals and companies. Her 'urgent optimism' concept is based on the hypothesis that if people feel an urgency to solve a problem and are optimistic about their ability to do so, they will succeed. She has found that optimism makes people likely to take positive action. In her book, *SuperBetter: a Revolutionary Approach to Getting Stronger, Happier, Braver and More Resilient — Powered by the Science of Games*[19], she describes in detail the three elements on which her 'urgent optimism' concept is built.

1. Mental Flexibility. The ability to resist being mentally blocked. The mental strength to recognise that everything could be different in the future and that things that seem impossible today can nonetheless be solved in the future.
2. Realistic Hope. The ability to balance positive and negative imagination; to know which risks and threats are important enough to worry about and which new solutions, technologies and positive actions are important to get excited about.
3. Future Power. The sense of having control over what the future will look like, by consciously initiating certain actions today.

Just when the pilots on Maverick's team no longer believed in the mission, he used the 'urgent optimism' model. By showing himself that it was possible to meet the sky-high demands of the mission, he relieved his team of mental blockage (mental flexibility) and allowed a realistic hope of success to emerge. The team then copied their leader's behaviour, and this instilled the belief in them that they would succeed in their mission (Future Power).

ARE THOSE THREE DAYS OF TOMORROWLAND REALLY THAT CRAZY?

Sometimes I am asked, 'Is all this positivism authentic? Is it realistic to exude a positive atmosphere all the time?' These are fair questions. I preface my response by explaining that I think authenticity is the most overblown marketing buzzword of recent years. Authenticity is not necessarily a good thing. Some people with extreme opinions can be very authentic, but this is not what the world is waiting for. Napoleon must have been very authentic, but was that a good thing?

Can you go overboard with positivity? The moment something very negative happens in your company, sector or environment, it should be acknowledged, but even so, you can deal with it in a positive way. Suppose your company makes a major mistake with a customer; this should of course be discussed with them. Admitting the mistake and responding to it empathetically is the first step. After that, you can see how things progress and formulate solutions tailored to the customer. There is (almost) always an opportunity to respond and communicate positively. President Zelenskyy is probably the best example of this theory. No matter how difficult the situation in his country is, he continues to communicate motivationally and positively.

Recently, I spoke with Bruno Vanwelsenaers, the CEO of the Tomorrowland Dance Festival in Belgium, globally regarded as one of the best dance festivals. People from all over the world flock to Belgium in July to enjoy the atmosphere, the music, the dancing and the people. Competition for tickets is so great that people must organise themselves in a highly professional way to get tickets. Groups of friends work together to ensure there is always someone on standby, ready to pounce on any tickets that become available.

When I spoke to Bruno, he posed a very interesting rhetorical question: *'Are the three days of Tomorrowland really that crazy?'* I was about to answer yes but he added, *'Or are those other 362 days of the year the crazy days?'* I looked at him, curious to know what his next comment would be. 'Well,' he continued, 'during those three days of Tomorrowland, everyone can be themselves. There is no racism, everyone is cheerful and tolerant. The event brings together 150,000 people from all kinds of cultures and backgrounds and every time it is one big party where everyone enjoys themselves. Maybe this is the world we should be striving for. Maybe we need to spread the Tomorrowland atmosphere to counteract the gloomy media reports and the polarisation of society.'

It is a very interesting point. Tomorrowland wants to spread that Tomorrowland feeling more widely in the future and not only during the festival. The organisers plan to focus on a wider range of entertainment in the coming years, for example by including the roller coaster at the Belgian amusement park, Plopsaland, and by offering even more music (with their own label and online community). It is the positive vibes of Tomorrowland that customers look forward to so much. According to Bruno, Tomorrowland's positivity has incredible potential because it is exactly what people are looking for today.

DO YOU AIM TO SELL PRODUCTS OR TO AIM FOR A POSITIVE CHANGE?

The team at Tomorrowland does more than sell tickets to their festival. They create unique memories and a 'wow' feeling that people look forward to for weeks. This begs an important question for you to ask yourself as an entrepreneur or manager: 'Are we only selling products/services, or can we also provide positive change in people's lives? Once we have found that positive change can we, like Tomorrowland, deploy it on different occasions or platforms?'

If the focus is only on selling products, then relationships with your customers will be transactional only. To become a beautiful, shinning diamond, you need deeper customer relationships. Ask yourself, 'Can our organisation create positive change in people's lives?'

Deepmind, one of Google's most advanced artificial intelligence divisions, surprised the world of science with the release of AlphaFold, in 2020. Alphafold is a super-powerful AI system that can predict the 3D structure of proteins based on their amino acid sequences. Understanding the 3D structure of proteins is a key capability for new drug discovery, and as such it has been widely regarded as one of the great biological challenges of our time. Predicting protein 3D structures has been a notoriously time intensive activity, in some cases requiring several years of research to determine the 3D folding pattern of a single protein. Alphafold can calculate a protein's *in vivo* confirmation in a few hours. You can imagine the financial value of an innovation that has reduced the time for an important step in drug discovery from several years to one afternoon. Each protein analysis could easily sell for hundreds of thousands of euros. In 2021, however, Deepmind decided to make the source code for AlphaFold and the 3D structures of one million proteins (almost every protein in the human body) available to the scientific community for free.[20]

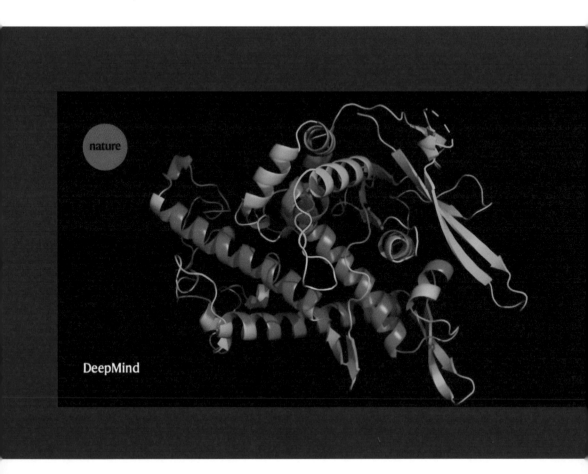

What will you do: sell products or create positive change in the world?

The people at Deepmind and Google thought the protein structures produced by AlphaFold were too valuable for the future of society to hide them behind a giant paywall. They are, of course, using the knowledge provided by AlphaFold for applications where they will realise commercial value.

Sometimes the best investment a company can make is to share concrete value with the world for free. Not only because this benefits the world, but also because this demonstrates the company's capabilities to the world. A lot of people have asked me why I share so much free content via my YouTube channel (www.youtube.com/stevenvanbelleghem). Co-presenters at conferences have called me crazy, saying things like, *'You put your full keynotes on your YouTube channel, and you share all your latest insights immediately in your weekly videos! So why should companies and event organisers invite you to speak live?'*

I have been sharing almost all my content via YouTube for more than eight years, but it was only on a long walk during the first few weeks of the COVID crisis that it dawned on me why I was motivated to do this. During the first lockdown, it saddened me to clear my agenda of all my scheduled presentations. I panicked at the knowledge that my business model had to evaporate for a prolonged period. On that walk, I realised that my mission is not to give keynote presentations. My mission is to make companies and individuals excited about the customer experience. I do this by creating content and sharing it with as many people as possible.

There are many platforms where I can share my knowledge, for example on my social media accounts and in my books. That fresh insight was a dose of energy that drove me towards sharing even more content. As a result, the videos on my YouTube channel have given millions of people a chance to engage with my ideas over the past few years. Hopefully, that has led to more satisfied customers for businesses in several places around the world. The videos have also advertised my capabilities, explained how I work and raised my credibility and profile with people that I might not have otherwise met who are very keen to meet with me. Bringing a story to a client in person is different from learning about it via a YouTube video.

Do I want to sell keynote presentations, or do I want to help there to be more satisfied customers in the world? It is the latter. One of the ways I do this is by selling myself as a keynote speaker, but distributing my content through other platforms also contributes to promoting myself. One is paid and the other is free. If I were to limit sharing my ideas and enthusiasm, I would bring less positive change and (I am convinced) would have sold fewer keynote presentations. The point is that trying to bring positive change helps your own brand and your own bottom line.

MRBEAST: POSITIVITY WITH IMPACT

Jimmy Donaldson, MrBeast, is as of this writing in mid 2023, the most popular YouTuber on the planet. I got to know about him thanks to my youngest son Mathis. I noticed that the same man kept showing up on Mathis' computer screen and eventually asked him who he was. It turned out to be MrBeast. I appointed Mathis as 'Vice President of MrBeast Research'. I am glad Mathis introduced me to MrBeast because his story is impressive.

MrBeast has more than 100 million followers on his channel and is currently the highest-earning YouTube star. In 2022, he earned USD 54 million just from the ads on his channel.[21] He started his YouTube career in 2011 by making classic gaming videos on Minecraft and later collaborated with Fortnite. He got his first boost in followers thanks to a very remarkable video, *Counting to 100,000*. The video attracted 100,000 followers in 24 hours. That was it! The video went viral and was the start of his amassing an extremely large group of followers. Sometime later, he decided to make someone happy by sharing revenue from his first sponsored video: he gave the proceeds (USD 10,000) to a randomly chosen person, a homeless man who stood by a traffic light all day begging for money.

He has continued the practice of donating much of his proceeds to his followers in the form of spectacular prizes and contests. Sharing his wealth makes him unique and it is the secret of his success. Some successful vloggers show their followers how cool it is to drive a Ferrari. **In contrast, followers of MrBeast can win a Ferrari.** I view MrBeast as the most successful quizmaster the world has ever seen. Many of his videos feature a creative competition where participants can win a plane or they must raise USD 1 million within two hours, or he gives random money to people at the supermarket. His videos have between 50 and

345 million viewers per video. One of his most popular videos is a remake of the Netflix series Squid Game. It shows how the profession of YouTubers has evolved in recent years. Many people envision YouTubers as young guys with an iPhone illuminated by a tiny lamp, but the reality is somewhat different. The MrBeast Squid Game video had a budget of USD 3.5 million[22], the contest winner took home just under USD 0.5 million, and every participant benefited. He creates positive change in the lives of his audience.

Eventually MrBeast's followers asked him to do something good for the environment. This was the start of the Beast Philanthropy channel. It has attracted over 10 million followers. The entire proceeds of this channel are donated to charity. Famous projects include planting 20 million trees and cleaning the world's most polluted beaches. The objective of the channel is not to have as many followers as possible but to make a positive change for followers and for society. MrBeast's story and approach is (literally) paying off. He has launched products over the last year, including the MrBeast Burger chain and Feastables, a chocolate line. MrBeast's company is valued at USD 1.5 billion.[23]

EVERYTABLE: WORKING FROM THE HEART

We are witnessing an evolution in how we work. In the past, most people worked with their hands. Today, most people work with their minds. In the future – if we want to make a difference in a digital world – people will have to work more from the heart. This is something a computer cannot do. The Top Gun Effect is about working from the heart. Enthusiasm, belief and positivity combine to create a solid foundation of customer relationships.

I was on a customer experience tour in Los Angeles with our inspiration company Nexxworks, where I had the opportunity to meet the team behind Every-Table. Their mission is to give every American the opportunity to eat a healthy meal at an affordable price. Healthy eating and health in general is a very important issue in America. Many people simply cannot afford healthy food. This is why Everytable shops are located mainly in lower-than-average-income neighbourhoods where the main food options are mostly fast food, a cheap way to eat but usually not healthy. Everytable offers an alternative: they sell pre-pared and healthy lunches, mainly a variety of salads and healthy sandwiches. Everytables prices their meals at 5 to 10% below the price of a Big Mac meal from a local McDonald's. This strategy meets their objective of offering target populations a healthier and cheaper alternative.

In addition, Everytable has some powerful tactics to further support the mis-sion. For example, if you go into an Everytable shop and the staff guesses that you can easily afford more than one of their lunches, they will ask if you are willing to buy a second lunch; not for yourself but for someone who would struggle to buy themselves lunch. If you agree, you are given a post-it note to hang outside the shop on one of their windows. When a homeless person, for example, passes by the window they can take the post-it note, enter the shop and receive the lunch you bought. This formula appeals to many people who want to help homeless people but often do not because they are shy about approaching them. This simple system is designed to lower the threshold for being charitable while helping people in need to eat more healthily.

Additionally, the owners of Everytable have devised a way to support their employees who live in the less affluent neighbourhoods where the shops are located: they can become co-owners of the shop where they work. Most franchises are not accessible for lower income people. Becoming a McDonald's franchisee, for example, requires a hefty down payment. As a result, most McDonald's restaurant owners are already successful entrepreneurs before they become franchisees. Everytable offers potential franchisees cheap loans, proper training and franchisees can qualify for government grants to help fund the project.

Everytable is a great example of a value-driven company. They have a very positive mission and try to make their positivity tangible for their customers and their employees in as many ways as possible. This is working from the heart in practice. It is easy to feel the Top Gun Effect in the customer service at Everytable.

CUSTOMERS DO NOT WANT PERFECTION – THEY WANT POSITIVE INTENTION

My goal for this chapter was to demonstrate the power of positivity. I have used my favourite analogy (Top Gun), presented key elements of the science behind positivity, given examples of companies that work with it and tried to impress upon you, the reader, the idea that enabling positive change for others will turn out positively for you as well. I hope you have felt my enthusiasm for this topic. At this point, you might be a little bit wary about so much positivity. You might be thinking, 'I am not perfect. I can have a bad day occasionally, can't I?'

Of course, you do not have to be perfect. We do not have to aspire to that. After all, there is no such thing as perfection. In fact, striving for perfection can block businesses, making it difficult to launch new initiatives. Also, customers do not expect perfection. What they do expect are positive intentions. If you ask a company a question and you have the impression that they are doing everything they can to help you – even if they never give you a satisfactory reply – most people can accept that. But all too often customers find that if their question is a little bit out of the norm, or falls a bit outside the company's existing processes, they will never receive a satisfactory answer. The lack of positive intentions can make a customer very frustrated.

The Top Gun Effect in customer experience is based on positive intention: we are going to do everything we can to make it right for the customer. We will not always succeed, but we want to make it a point of honour to at least try. We know we are not perfect, but we are still going to try to make a positive change in our customers' lives. If you have that mindset, then you are using the power of the Top Gun Effect. You can implement the Top Gun Effect by adding small surprises to your customer experience (e.g., JetBlue), or a fun physical element (e.g., Magic Castle). The strongest examples of the Top Gun Effect take place when that positivity is at the company's core (MrBeast, Everytable, GAS).

Adding the Top Gun Effect to your customer experience is the first step towards a brighter diamond. It is important that customers and employees know what you stand for and that they can feel and see that positive intention in action.

The strongest examples of the ***Top Gun Effect*** take place if that positivity really is at the core of the company.

CONCRETE CUSTOMER EXPERIENCE TIPS FROM THIS CHAPTER:

1. When communicating externally, always make it a positive message. Even if there is bad news to deliver, make sure there is a positive story attached to it.
2. Never moan about your own problems to your customers. They have 0% interest in your problems.
3. The media is often looking for negative stories about people and about companies with problems. Do not be tempted contribute to this.
4. Compliment your customers. Highlight the good things you see in your customers.
5. Send customers a spontaneous gift when something nice has happened in their lives.
6. Send handwritten cards to several customers every week to congratulate or thank them.
7. Send a personal note along with your invoice, so that your relationship with them does not become impersonal. Make even your invoices amusing.
8. Respond to your customers' social media posts: congratulate them, wish them well.
9. Radiate optimism, positivity and energy. You are looking forward to today!
10. Come up with a 'caring and sharing' philosophy that suits your company. How can you facilitate donations from your customers two people in need?
11. Create a 'Feel Good Mails' folder in your mailbox. Every time you receive positive feedback from a client via e-mail, you can put the e-mail in that folder. On a gloomy day, just scroll through those 'feel food' e-mails and you will have the energy to make customers happy again.
12. Striving for perfection can block very valuable CX ideas and experiments. Realise that customers do not want perfection but do want positive intent.
13. Think about the corners of your mouth. Research how to make your customers smile. That feel-good factor, what I call the Top Gun Effect, is so powerful. It can sometimes happen even with very small measures such as with a funny message in a confirmation email.

CHAPTER 3

THE CIRCLE OF INFLUENCE

'WITH GREAT POWER COMES **GREAT RESPONSIBILITY!**'

SPIDERMAN

ANGEL CITY FC

Anyone who knows me knows that I am a big Club Brugge supporter. I had never watched another football team play live until I was in Los Angeles on an 'inspiration trip' in March 2023. **It was then that I saw Angel City FC play in a practice match against Club América FC. I was mightily impressed by the Angel City team.** There were 19.000 people in the stadium that night, more people than David Beckham drew when he played in the MLS league for LA Galaxy in that stadium. Quite a feat for a team that has only been in existence since 2020 and played their first match in 2022.

It is a unique story! Angel City is a professional women's football team founded by some very influential women such as Natalie Portman, Serena Williams and Jennifer Garner. The team was founded with a mission: to promote gender equality in sport, on and off the field. They want to use the power of sport to bring about a positive change in society.

They measure their success in part by their ability to secure sponsorship deals as big as the male teams. The shirt sponsor of a men's team in the US pays an average of USD 2.5 million to advertise on the team's jerseys, while for women's teams the average is USD 1 million. The difference is attributed to the greater exposure and media coverage for men's teams. Angel City managed to secure a USD 2.5 million deal, mainly due to the power of their influencer community who, among other things, post photos of themselves wearing jerseys on social media. Ten percent of the sponsorship money goes straight back to the community in support of projects related to gender equality and women's rights.

Angel City team members also earn more than members of other women's teams. This allows them to attract better players and increases the chances of sporting success. In return, players are expected to not only play good football but also to actively participate in promoting the mission. Players make themselves available for attendance at gender equality events and promote the mission on social media. Can you imagine the positive spiral this creates? A strong mission, consistent actions, spreading the story … in the end, all of this has generated the financial and sporting success that enables Angel City FC to empower their mission.

The team's impressive and inspiring story has instant appeal to many people. A wide range of mostly female investors is financing Angel City. Rather than depending on a small number of large shareholders, Angel City's funding strategy has been to attract a broad community of investors, including a wide range of celebrities and influential female investors that increase the depth and reach of the club's community work and mission. Typically, each investor contributes a modest amount, limiting the likelihood that investors will need to cash in at short notice with the effect of stabilising the club's financial position. For many of these ce-

lebrities, Angel City is a 'hobby' investment. They are motivated to be actively involved and spread the club's story. The club and members of the club's circle of influence have successfully used social media to boost awareness, as did their strategy to play in every local football match they could find at the early stage of their formation. **'No event was too big or too small for us,' we heard during a presentation of their story.** They sought out fans everywhere and the benefit is clear to see. As of 2023, the stadium is completely sold out for the next five to six years, and their community work is producing results.

In this chapter, I want to show you how you can manage your company's circle of influence with great impact: to add value to society in a focused way while remaining as true to your company's core objectives as possible. Your company's circle of influence includes your internal and external stakeholders and those who may be affected, in both a positive and a negative way, by your company's products, services, policies and actions. This can include employees as well as customers, investors and board members, industry partners and competitors, government agencies and consultants. If we examine Angel City's success through this perspective, they are fighting for women's rights by launching a unique women's football team while leading by example.

Angel City FC is a good example of the success delivered by having a clear focus and mission, translated into effective strategies and tactics to achieve Angel City's goals, a creative financing strategy and recruitment strategy, tangible and measurable outcomes from the execution of the mission statement and a carefully managed and motivated circle of influence.

Throughout this chapter, you will see that three elements are important: add value – focus – and stay close to the core!

THERE IS NO MORE SWITZERLAND

'If you are not part of the solution, you are part of the problem!' This observation by Simon Mainwaring has stayed with me. Simon is a good friend. He is also an excellent speaker and inspirational author of *We First* and *Lead with Me*. He is an opinion leader on how large companies can create value for society and be successful brands at the same time. Being neutral in a social debate is becoming increasingly difficult. Neutral Switzerland is slowly but surely disappearing in the business world. Being neutral is no longer the safe option. After all, if you do not share an opinion, part of the market will think you are in 'the wrong' camp. If a company is not visibly striving to address a problem, it runs the risk of being seen as a company that is exacerbating the problem.

When a group of frustrated Trump supporters stormed the US Capitol in January 2020, the world watched this unreal spectacle in astonishment. Many brands were unsure how to respond. About half of Americans were pro-Trump, the other half anti. Condemning the riots could have gone down the wrong way with a large group of consumers. The deodorant brand Axe, part of Unilever, was one of those brands that did not react to the riots. The day after the riots, a picture appeared in the media of an empty canister of Axe on the capital grounds. One of the rioters was clearly a fan of Axe and wanted to keep their sweat under control. Inevitably, the brand was dragged into the story even if they did not want to be. You may think you can stay neutral, but the context can change quickly.

Steering clear of social challenges is becoming increasingly difficult because of perceptions and often for economic reasons. Climate issues are directly linked to the operation of almost every company. Topics such as racism, discrimination and diversity are also high on the agenda of every board of directors. Even in a war, companies take sides. McDonald's departure from the Russian market in the wake of Russia's attack on Ukraine sent the clear message that they support Ukraine.

Through my consultancy work, I have seen companies struggle with how to address societal problems. They have opinions, but often find that the safest option is to say nothing (externally). After all, it is usually recommended that companies should put a positive spin on all their external communications. If a company has an opinion on a particular social issue, there is a 100% guarantee that part of the market will hold an opposing view. And this is a point of debate within companies: should they risk contradicting the opinions of part of their customers to remain true to the company's values?

You may remember the discussion around the 'one love' bracelet during the 2022 Qatar World Cup. In the first week of the World Cup, FIFA abruptly banned team captains from wearing the armband. Perhaps the Qatar regime urged FIFA to ban the symbol of 'love for all' from the tournament and their country. Those who wore the bracelets would receive a yellow card and perhaps additional sporting sanctions. There were supporters and opponents, but finally, everyone decided not to wear the bracelet and to focus on the sporting event.

I understood their choice, but it reminded me of the discussion in 2016 that surrounded Colin Kaepernick – a member of the San Francisco 49ers NFL team at the time. He was the first athlete in history to kneel during a national anthem to protest racism and discrimination. Today, this is a well-known symbol of silent protest. But in 2016, Kaepernick's action created a full-blown controversy that led to his dismissal. Moreover, no other team offered him a contract. Only Nike picked him up and soon launched a high-profile campaign. The message was: **'Believe in something, even if it means sacrificing everything!' An impressive message to this day!** But many Americans could not swallow it. They thought kneeling was a disgraceful sign of disrespect for the US flag. Consequently, the day after the campaign launch, the internet was teeming with people burning their Nike products. Nike, however, did not back down but instead launched a new and exciting campaign with the message, 'How to burn our products safely!' In other words: you may disagree, you may even burn our products, but know that we will not change our minds. There is a big difference between Nike's fortitude compared with the reaction of the football teams that played in Qatar.

Meanwhile, people's expectations that companies acknowledge and address their social responsibilities are becoming a priority. The under 30s' opinion is clear: 77% of Americans aged 18 – 29 and 52% of those aged 45 – 59 expect companies to operate in an environmentally sustainable way.[24] Seventy-two percent of the younger group want companies to focus on long-term benefits for society rather than pursuing short-term profits. This figure drops to 47% for the older group. Disappointment with the performance of companies in sustainability is on the rise: 67% of those aged 45+ – believe that companies are underperforming, and that number rises to 86% for 18 – 29 years old. Fourteen percent of the younger group believe most companies have a focus on delivering long-term social benefits versus 24% of the older group. **Overall, it can be said that there is a clear trend towards increased expectations in society for better adjusted moral compasses of organisations.**

YOUR CIRCLE OF INFLUENCE

New societal expectations create opportunities to increase companies' social influence. Historically, organisations acted primarily in their own business interest. Decisions were made as necessary to optimise results and improve market position. Developments within a corporation's industry were closely monitored. Companies tried to influence these developments to their advantage through lobbying or active membership in industry associations. They also followed global developments within their business sector and assessed its impact on their bottom line. In other words, corporate social awareness and influence was limited.

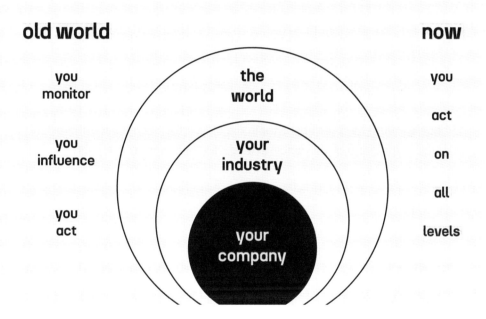

Today, companies seek to operate in a way that makes financial sense, but also in a socially responsible manner. Naturally, managers and entrepreneurs want to act in their company's interest. An increasingly popular solution to achieve this is close collaboration between competitors to create win-wins for whole sectors. Competitors are even organising joint events to enable industry-wide awareness around a particular theme. Ford and Volkswagen have been working together on electric vehicles since 2019, for example, and their collaboration was expanded in 2022.

The biggest change in recent years is found at the level of social responsibility with companies taking increasingly active roles to make a difference. This is most visible in climate change. A recent study by Deloitte shows that climate change is the top priority for business leaders in 2023. Climate change ranks higher in terms of priority than geopolitical tensions, logistics challenges and talent shortages.[25] Many companies have recently faced the consequences of climate change. Factories have been flooded, severe fires have made factories inaccessible and increasingly severe storms have made it impossible for customers to access shops. Companies in China and Germany have suffered hydropower problems or supply chain delays due to lack of water in lakes, reservoirs and waterways. Chances are very high that you have encountered a (negative) consequence of climate change within your own company in the past 12 months. Everyone is dealing with the impact of climate change. Business leaders are starting to realise that it is in their own economic interest to act. Moreover, the market is also increasingly demanding it (see above). More and more companies are imposing high demands on their suppliers, with 59% demanding products made from sustainable materials.

Companies must be clear about their social role to become beautiful bright diamonds. Their circle of influence extends further than in the past. This is an opportunity to use the positivity that the Top Gun Effect can offer to create social added value, which is of increasing importance for customers and for employees.

FILOU & FRIENDS WANTS EVERY CHILD TO PLAY IN SUSTAINABLE CLOTHING

I have had the opportunity to work closely with Rudi and Emile Maes, in recent years. Rudi is the founder of Filou & Friends, a popular Belgian children's clothing brand. Emile is his son who has been running the company with him for many years. Rudi's wife, Sophie Decubber, has been the creative director since the company began.

Rudi contacted me in late 2020 after reading my previous book, *The Offer You Can't Refuse*. He was overjoyed. They were convinced that the philosophy I presented in my book would help them take their business to the next level. Their goal is to become as sustainable and recyclable a brand as possible. Their mission is to ensure that every child will be able to play in high quality and fashionable clothes. To fulfil their mission, the garments must be made in a sustainable way and their quality must provide great durability so that the clothes can be passed on to other children.

A wonderful thing about the Maes family is that working as sustainably as possible is second nature to them. Sustainability really is in these people's DNA. Initially, they only sold their brand through children's clothing shops. Over time, they decided to sell only through their own Filou & Friends shops and web-shop so they could control the entire value chain. Practically everything is done in-house including the creation of fabric design and manufacturing, patterns and samples. The raw materials and manufacture are always of high quality and durability, allowing families to pass clothing on to younger brothers or sisters.

Filou & Friends' circle of influence goes further than you might imagine. Because they produce high-quality sustainable products, their clothing has a long lifespan resulting in a lower impact on the environment. This presents many opportunities to further increase the brand's positive social contribution and further reduce the environmental impact of their products. These were the beginnings of the Filou Forever brand.

The Filou Forever business model is as follows: customers are invited to return garments to a Filou & Friends shop when they no longer have a use for them. If the garment passes the Filou & Friends quality control exam, the customer receives a partial refund of its purchase price in the form of a voucher to buy new garments and the pre-worn quality-controlled product is added to the Filou Forever collection. People with modest means are then able to buy high-quality beautiful and durable clothing for their children. Filou Forever helps the company to make their mission statement even more tangible: every child should be able to play in beautiful and sustainable clothing. Rudi puts it very nicely himself: *'Our target group is young children, the future of tomorrow. As a company, you therefore want to effectively give those young people a future by consciously opting for sustainability and recyclability.'*[26]

≡ **FILOU & FRIENDS**   Q | NL ⌄   ⦿ login   🛍

Home   FOREVER

FILOU FOREVER
Second hand approved by Filou & Friends
Lees hier meer over Filou Forever

The Maes family's ambition is to grow the company further based on their razor-sharp mission statement. Their strategy impacts their own business and society; they have created a circle of influence that has been integrated into their way of working. 'We want to do good, by doing the right thing,' Rudi says. They are now thinking about ways to expand their positive influence. Possible new business models include clothing repair or clothing rental. Rudi dreams of a Filou & Friends fund where they can bring their mission to life in a broader social sphere.

'THE EARTH IS OUR ONLY SHAREHOLDER!'

In September 2022, Yvon Chouinard, founder of the US based outdoor clothing and supplies company, Patagonia, decided to convert his company (turnover of about USD 1 billion between 2017 and 2020[27]) into a non-profit organisation rather than going public or selling the company. The goal? To make their already positive impact on the climate even greater. In an open letter, the company's 83-year-old founder explained his reasoning very clearly: *'The earth is now our only shareholder! … It has been almost 50 years since we started this experiment of doing business in a responsible way and we are really just getting started.'*

Chouinard's decision will not change the way the company is run. Patagonia will continue to market beautiful, sporty and sustainable clothing and try to do so as successfully as possible. What has changed is the structure of the company. A non-profit trust fund – Patagonia Purpose Trust – owns 2% of Patagonia but has 100% voting rights. The purpose of the fund is to guard Patagonia's values and independence. The shop has become a non-profit and owns 98% of the trust find but has no voting rights. The non-profit's mission is to channel Patagonia's profits into the fund. These profits are used in their entirety for the fight against climate change. On average, about USD 100 million a year will go to the fund. The money will not be used for charitable donations. Even before these changes, Patagonia had already donated 1% of their sales to non-profit organisations. The money from the fund is being used to make their influence felt in a much greater sphere. The aim is to influence and co-direct climate policy. The Chouinard family is taking a lead role in the fund to guard the founder's legacy. **'I actually never wanted to be in business,'** Yvon Chouinard said in an interview in the *Wall Street Journal.* **'But I continue to invest in Patagonia because it is my means of achieving something good for the world.'**[28]

WHEN DIGITAL PRODUCTS BECOME GEOPOLITICAL WEAPONS, DOES INFLUENCE GO TOO FAR?

The circle of influence of organisations expands year after year. Today, companies have a voice in almost every social topic and their actions are often more impactful than governments realise. Real climate change will come from the companies that will raise the bar for one another far higher than those imposed by governments. Market and employee pressure will motivate them. The economic benefits of companies using their influence in a positive way has become more tangible in recent years.

The crystal-clear question is: are there limits to corporate influence on society? Would it be dangerous if some companies develop too large a circle of influence? The line between corporations and governments can sometimes become blurred.

Consider the US government's push to ban TikTok (I am writing this in March 2023; it may have happened by the time this book is published). The government's advice to users was clear: delete your TikTok account, buy a new phone and never use TikTok again. **Many US politicians are alarmed that TikTok might be a weapon used by the Chinese government as a tool for spying on a mass scale. It would be the best Trojan horse in history.** You give a population a tool so addictive that just about everyone installs it on their phone and uses it daily, and you use the tool to access the data on those phones. It looks like a scenario from one of the three Romy Bell technology thrillers I wrote in the past few years (*Eternal, The Upgrade, High Betrayal*), but it could well be reality.

Many people were shocked by the results of an analysis that compared Western and Chinese TikTok content.[29] The Chinese version is much more child-friendly than the West's. In China, most of the content is educational, such as videos on science that educate children in a fun way. Moreover, there is a time limit of 40 minutes per day on the app. Compare that to the West where the app has no time limit, and the content cannot be described as particularly edifying. TikTok's circle of influence in China is clearly positive and adds value to their youth; its influence in the West is less clear, to say the least. One telling example of the effect that such media has on the young is that if you ask Western children what they want to be when they grow up the top answer is an influencer, while Chinese children dream of becoming astronauts.[30]

What if governments (and therefore citizens) were to become completely dependent on one company, for instance to ensure their security? Can the power of one company or one person go too far? Let us go back to the beginning of the war between Russia and Ukraine. Shortly after the Russians invaded the country, Elon Musk jumped into the breach on behalf of civilians and the military by giving them permanent access to the internet via his Starlink technology, a network of internet access satellites. In March 2022, about two weeks after the invasion, I was able to see for myself how quickly and impressively the team at Starlink was at work. During a visit to Los Angeles, I had the chance to visit the Starlink and SpaceX factory. Large hangars were filled with Starlink boxes (the receivers) with 'Ukraine' written in big letters on them. In the following weeks, Starlink became an important tool for the Ukrainian military. All communication at the front soon went through Musk's satellites. Well done, Elon Musk!

Yet, some people were disconcerted when a few months later Musk posted his proposal for a peace plan on his favourite channel, Twitter. He suggested that a lasting peace could be possible if Ukraine accepted Russia's annexation of Crimea. Ukraine would not become a member of NATO under Musk's plan and the division of land between Ukraine and Russia would be decided via referendums in the affected regions.

Many Ukrainians were furious and asserted that the message seemed to come straight from Putin. So, what was the overall social benefit of Musk's peace plan via Twitter? His escapade could be written off as one more folly from Musk. But there is more to it. Musk had a big influence on Ukraine's military due to his contribution of Starlink. Without the internet access it provides, Ukraine's position would be much more tenuous. So Starlink has a clear positive circle of influence.

The downside (danger) is the unpredictability of the driver of that circle of influence. At one point in 2022, for example, Musk complained that he would have to begin charging for Starlink services to Ukraine. The implication was that the US would be expected to pay to continue the service, causing extreme nervousness in the halls of the Pentagon. Risk is inherent when the circle of influence is largely dependent on one person. This story underlines one of the important roles of a board: to ensure that the company's values are clearly described and that the company's actions are aligned with these.

SEWA: SOMETIMES IT IS IN THE CULTURE!

'In America, entrepreneurs want to build great companies; in India, entrepreneurs want to build a better society.' This is one of the most haunting quotes from an interview conducted by our company, Nexxworks, with India expert observer Shayamal Vallabhjee.[31] Western companies are discovering how to manage their circle of influence and implementing this step by step, while in other markets – India, for instance – it is in the genes of society.

Indian social entrepreneurship is deeply rooted in the concept of Sewa, meaning service. Indian people will always share with others, even if they have very little themselves. The Sewa tradition is why so many successful new Indian companies aim to build social value. Tata Steel, an Indian B2B company over 100 years old, donates 60% of its profits to education or medical charitable funds. Hindustan Unilever Limited (a subsidiary of Unilever) gives 25% of every penny they earn back to the community. Giving is part of doing business. However, the Sewa tradition goes beyond the support of charitable funds. For many Indian companies, giving back to society is ingrained in their business models.

Unacademy, an online education platform, aims to further democratise education in India. India has already made great strides in education, but there is still room for improvement. Only 61% of 3 to 5-year-olds were attending school in India in 2020, versus 83% in OECD countries.[32]

Unacademy was started by engineering student Gaurav Munjal in 2015 as a YouTube channel. He made short videos to help his fellow students prepare for exams. In late 2015, he and two of his friends launched the Unacademy app with free interactive content. It is an open platform app allowing others such as teachers and students to create educational content. Two years later, the platform had more than 1 million users, 5,000 registered tutors and offered more than 40,000 courses.[33] Today, millions of people use the app and new classes are continually being added. In essence, Unacademy supports India's existing school system. Of course, people who do not attend school can use Unacademy to educate themselves.

There are examples in other countries of traditions like Sewa, where making positive change for people and the planet is ingrained in the culture. In many other countries, big steps still need to be taken. As the world becomes more global, consumers will have more choice when deciding which companies they will patronise or work with, increasing the importance for companies to have a clear position on social challenges.

TOMS SHOES IS HARD ON ITSELF

The Sewa principle is not really known, let alone established in Western markets. Yet there are Western companies where adding value for society is one of their core values. Think of the earlier examples of Filou & Friends and Patagonia. Toms Shoes is another such company. In 2006, the company was launched from their Los Angeles headquarters. Its founder, Blake Mycoskie, started the company after a visit to Argentina. There he saw how children often walked the streets without shoes. Blake's goal was to solve the problem of lack of footwear among poor children by starting a shoe brand himself. Toms slogan 'One for One' became famous very quickly. For each pair of shoes purchased, Toms donated a pair of shoes to an underprivileged child. The circle of influence was very tangible for customers and is at the core of what they do as a company. The 'One for One' concept remains strongly linked to the brand and has been the driver of awareness and growth.

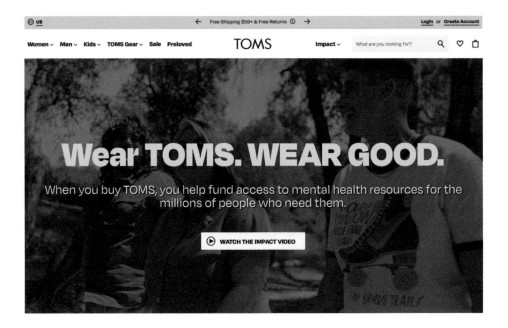

Toms CMO, Amy Smith, along with the rest of the management team, decided to discontinue the 'One for One' concept in 2019 to be replaced by a new scheme chosen for its potential to have broader impact. They will continue to donate as much to charity, namely 1/3 of profits, as they did with the 'One for One' principle, but from 2019 they have focused on mental health through charitable donations.

In March 2023, I had the chance to visit their Los Angeles headquarters to learn more about their story. It was clear that they had somewhat underestimated the challenges of the switch from 'One for One' to 'we support mental health issues by donating 1/3 of our profits to social programmes'. **I imagine that you can sense the differences between these two programmes. The 'One for One' concept is very simple and very close to their core,** while the new story is hard to explain and has no link to their core. This means that the impact of donations can feel less tangible to customers. This is unfortunate. Supporting mental health is very important and is a noble cause. But the link to Toms story has been lost, making it harder for them to realise benefits.

It is a shame that Toms is having difficulty selling their new social impact story. It demonstrates that even with a circle of influence in place companies can make it too difficult to assert their influence, lowering their impact. In Toms case, their circle of influence has been diminished because there is no synergy between their core values, products and social activity.

EVERY CHALLENGE IS A POTENTIAL OPPORTUNITY

Most companies do not have a circle of influence emanating from within their core and must look for a way to make a difference. Today, the market is flooded with Sustainable Development Goal (SDG) reports in which companies try to score on as many aspects as possible. Employees put hours of their time into such reports. They are posted on the company's website where they are read by only a small handful of enthusiasts. My feeling is that, for the moment, most companies should plan and wait before launching a new SDG activity. It seems smarter to me to focus on one or two SDGs and find a way to make them fit your core. Having done that, it becomes credible to communicate your decision to work on the SDG and organise actions around it. Ultimately, the point of your investment in the circle of influence is to have both social and market impact. If you work a small amount on several SDGs, no one will notice your contribution. If you can focus efforts in a smart way, you optimise impact.

Food waste is a big problem in the United States. It is believed that 30% to 40% of the food produced is thrown away,[34] an insane percentage. The UN's SDG12 initiative aims to halve food waste on a per person basis by 2030 and condiments producer Hellmann's wants to play a role. Particularly known for their mayonnaise, they have launched a mayonnaise made with rescued eggs, those that would otherwise be thrown away because they have minor imperfections such as small cracks in their shells. Mayonnaise is an ideal binding agent for making delectable dishes out of leftovers; Hellmann's have published a companion cookbook of inspirational recipes created from leftovers. The company has tackled a concrete problem by using a logical extension of their core product line. This is a good example of how to tackle a social problem while creating a new business opportunity.

WHAT IF YOU GET CAUGHT WITH YOUR HAND IN THE BISCUIT JAR?

McDonald's, Coca-Cola and Starbucks are some of the many Western companies that abandoned their operations in Russia upon the outbreak of the war in Ukraine.[35] Initially, Heineken also promised to withdraw completely from Russia, but as of March 2023, they had yet to make good on their promise. Rather, they expanded operations to fill the vacuum left by other beverage producers. According to Heineken's market update, their Russian operations recorded strong growth in 2022 on the back of the launch of 61 new products in record time and a 720,000 hectolitre increase in the volume of soft drinks and beer sold. Because Guinness, Coca-Cola and Pepsi dropped out of the market, Heineken launched a Guinness copycat beer and a product they have named Royal Cola.

Heineken was caught with their hand in the biscuit jar. Their actions led to a media storm in their home market of the Netherlands. I could make harsh comments about Heineken, but it is likely that others have also reached their hand into the biscuit jar; it is just that Heineken was caught. **What should companies do in such cases? There is only one option: practise extreme transparency.**

A few days after the media furore erupted, Heineken reported their version of the facts, saying that Heineken-labelled products had effectively disappeared from the Russian market. They said the head office had given the Russian branch permission to develop and launch new products to avoid bankruptcy at the Russian operation, which would have put 1.800 people on the street. They said their aim is to sell the Russian operation, but it is taking longer than expected. Some of you will find this a credible explanation; others may find this typically obtuse management-speak. It was the extreme transparency the market was waiting for. Heineken should have they used their circle of influence to communicate with extreme transparency from the start. This could have put a quick stop to the media storm. Heineken may have found it initially difficult to explain their actions but if one is honest from the outset, people are more likely to forgive mistakes.

Transparency takes courage. You explain where you are doing well and not so well. Transparency also means that society can hold you to account for your promises and the extent of your progress towards fulfilling them.

ATTRACTING TALENT REQUIRES COMMITMENT AND TRANSPARENCY

Seventy four percent of millennials say they feel most fulfilled if their job offers them opportunities to make a positive impact on social and environment issues and 70% say that these opportunities also increase their loyalty to employers. Moreover, 51% would not even take a job with a company that lacked strong social and environmental sustainability policies.
Deloitte's 2016 report on talent retention showed that two-thirds of millennials would quit their jobs if they felt their employer was only profit-oriented.[36] It is clear: social engagement is a driver for talent attraction and retention. The circle of influence is not only important because of its impact on customers: its impact on employees can be even more important.

Transparent communication is the most important characteristic of a company to gain the confidence of employees (and all other stakeholders). Fifty-four percent of employees say that full transparency creates confidence that the company is doing the right thing.[37] Top talent expects regular updates on objectives, progress and the results of social impact projects. Employees can accept that everything is not perfect, but they do expect openness about plans and processes and the associated challenges and successes. They want to be involved in helping the company achieve its social goals.

Companies that consider their circle of influence when planning their social strategies and communicate those strategies openly are best positioned to become beautiful and sparkling diamonds. The positivity of the Top Gun Effect and the intention to make a difference in the social sphere are both part of making the diamond bright for customers and employees. Everyone will understand what you stand for and be excited about it.

CIRCLES OF INFLUENCE
AND THE BOTTOM LINE

Management that considers the effects of their business practices on members within their circle of influence can also benefit the bottom line. Employees who judge their organisation as environmentally and socially responsible report better mental health and are more productive, correlating with 31% higher productivity and 37% higher sales.

HOW TO BEGIN?

Too many companies only tick boxes and do not take action with sincerity. Are we making sincere efforts around sustainability? Check! And what about efforts with SDGs? Check! Is there an 'About Us' section on our website that describes our contributions to society? Check!

As I mentioned when discussing SDGs, (too) many resources go into ticking checkboxes. Customers (and employees) care little about checklists and box ticking. As well-intentioned as this may be, just ticking boxes will not have an impact in the company nor the marketplace.

A focused vision and goals that are not only intentions but actioned results result in a diamond with clarity. Think like Hellmann's: how can our strength address one of the SDGs? Focus helps to make intentions and plans of action clear to customers and employees.

CONCRETE CUSTOMER EXPERIENCE TIPS FROM THIS CHAPTER:

1. Identify what your company can do on a social level that is compatible with the sector in which you operate. (e.g., Can an insurance broker help make the municipality safer for cyclists?)

2. Define which social issues suit your company and formulate a positive opinion that you are prepared to support. When relevant, you can share that opinion about them, not with the intent of creating polarisation but to make a positive contribution.

3. List the efforts that your company is making regarding sustainability and define how you can communicate this best. Also identify which actions are still missing.

4. If you support charities, find a way to relate your choice of charities to your core values, products or services so that you can tell a positive story about your company. Easy to understand stories that have a clear relationship to your core business and values are best.

5. Look at the list of United Nation's SDGs and ask yourself: which ones relate best to our mission and products, and which of these is one where we could make a tangible difference? Then you can take the appropriate action.

6. If there is negative news about your company, be transparent in your communication.

7. What do you want to do: sell products or create positive change in the world? The demands of your business must be considered, but your business will benefit if you make a positive mindset a feature of the customer experience.

8. As you expand your circle of influence as a brand and speak out on social challenges, you may meet with challenges, from outside and inside your circle of influence. Be brave, like Nike was with Colin Kaepernick.

CHAPTER 4

BELIEVE!

'BELIEVE!'

TED LASSO

WECRASHED!

One of my favourite television series of the past few years is undoubtedly *We-Crashed* on Apple TV. The docudrama tells the curious story of entrepreneur Adam Neumann, the co-founder of WeWork, and his wife Rebekah Neumann. It shows what it was like behind the scenes at WeWork and how Adam Neumann thought and acted. At times it is too insane to believe, although insiders say the series is very realistic. Ex-employees recognise some scenes almost word for word.

Adam Neumann founded WeWork with business associate Miguel McKelvey in 2010. Adam Neumann was CEO of the company until 2019. During that time, WeWork became one of the fastest-growing start-ups the world has ever seen. At one point, the company was valued at USD 47 billion. Neumann was ousted as CEO and new management was brought in on the back of a failed IPO in 2019.

Given WeWork's initially spectacular rate of growth and robust valuation, one would expect that WeWork was a high-technology software or hardware company that had invented something unique and managed to market it in a successful way. That is not the case at all. WeWork rents flexible office space: a business model that has existed for many years and is hardly novel. IWG, operating as Regus in the market, is an example of a long-term player in WeWork's sector. At the time that WeWork floated their IPO, Regus was turning a profit, but WeWork was not.

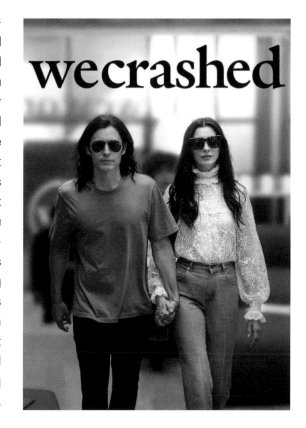

Yet at that time IWG was valued at only 10% of WeWork's valuation.[38] WeWork may have been regarded by some as less boring than its competitors, but their core offering is quite similar. Yet the valuation of WeWork was disproportionate to its potential. So how did the company get such a valuation? The answer is simple: Adam Neumann is an unimaginably good salesman. He can get people super excited and managed to convey his stories in a very convincing way. He encouraged people to believe that he was working on something unique.

Neumann told everyone the story of the We-Generation: a segment of the population, especially younger people, who wanted more than just a job. When Neumann was still at the helm, he described the WeWork environment as a place where people went to have fun, not simply to work. Neumann referred to clients as members and positioned the company as building communities where young people could share their experiences and philosophise about life while doing their jobs. WeWork was pitched as much more than office space: WeWork was a philosophy. Neumann proclaimed this message everywhere and managed to get major, experienced investors like SoftBank on board as investors.

Neumann resisted paying employees their full salaries for years with the promise of making a lot of money if WeWork went public. Despite the poor financial results, which would only have been shared with his investors prior to the IPO, Neumann managed to keep this story going for almost a decade.

The company's financials were made public in preparation for the IPO, revealing the weakness of the financial results and Neumann's dubious business practices. The bubble burst, the IPO was pulled, and Neumann was kicked out by his board of directors. The whole Neumann story was one big fantasy that a lot of smart and experienced people went along with. Neumann seemingly did not have to convince people, they believed him. This means that despite never being able to lead the company into profitability, disloyal stock sales, not paying people their full salaries, massaging the balance sheets and more,[39] people believed in him. **Once people believe you, they will usually go along with your story. It is not about convincing people; it is about instilling belief.**

Do not misunderstand; I am not suggesting that you fabricate a story and use it to influence your employees or the market. Schemes like Neumann's inevitably go wrong sooner or later. My message in this chapter is: do not try to convince your employees that you are customer-centric, make them believe you are!

WHO BELIEVES THESE PEOPLE ANYMORE?

As a conference, seminar and workshop speaker, I am regularly invited to internal company meetings. Very often, my assignment is to endorse the company's strategy and get employees excited about it. I love doing that but often the well-meaning intentions of such meetings completely miss the mark.

Picture it: you are an employee of a company, and you get an invitation from top management to attend a meeting about customer experience. The CEO and an external specialist will speak. You and many other employees are excited by the topic and sign up for the meeting. *'Nice, talking about customer experience for an afternoon. Super,'* people think. By a few minutes before the presentation starts, the room has filled up nicely. Everyone is filled with anticipation. The CEO takes the floor, and everyone sits on the edge of their seats. Everyone looks forward to the CEO's new ideas to make customers happier.

'Before we start with the customer experience part, I want to give you a quick update on our financial results and how far we deviate from our targets,' the CEO goes on and on, overwhelming employees with 10 minutes of tables, graphs, red and green numbers and arrows pointing hither and thither. Not a word is spoken about customers, the CEO is fixated on how much above or below the company is from the annual target. Finally, the CEO reaches the end of his presentation and finishes by saying, *'I thought it was important to give everyone an update on our performance. Oh yes, and now we can move on to the bit about the customer. I give the floor to our speaker.'* I can feel the vibes in the room change. The enthusiasm dies down. Top management think the numbers are most important, but these people were there for something else.

By starting the meeting like this, the CEO immediately undermined the belief that customer focus will become the company's priority from now on. The theme you start the meeting with and how much time you spend on it will indicate where the focus truly lies.

A few months ago, I was invited to Milan by Antonio Gianno, Chief Commercial Officer of Hoya Surgical Optics, to support him in presenting the new customer strategy. This meeting was the perfect example of how it should be done. Antonio started the meeting with Hoya's customer strategy. He gave an impressive 45-minute speech in which he explained in a very convincing and motivating way about the changes needed in the coming years to improve the customer experience. I then took the floor to further heighten people's enthusiasm. By the end of the meeting, everyone was not only convinced that the new strategy was needed, but they also believed in Antonio's sincerity and determination make it a success. That was not down to me, but to Antonio's clever build-up in this meeting.

Too many top managers and entrepreneurs underestimate the impact of small decisions and choices in the process of getting people excited about a new strategy or project. If you want to get people excited about a customer-centric culture, try to focus your message on that. Everything else is noise and creates the impression that you do not believe it is as important as you pretend.

Most companies have a PowerPoint slide on which customer focus (or some variant) is described as one of its core values, while everyone realises that this message has not gone any further than that PowerPoint slide. The desire and intention to be customer-centric often remains, but the action fails to materialise. In my experience, the main reason for inaction is that employees simply do not believe that their managers are sincere.

YES, YES, DO, BUT REMEMBER...

I will never forget it. I had the opportunity to conduct several days of workshops for a large European company operating in the construction industry. The marketing director was keen to take the next step in customer focus. After two days of very enthusiastic brainstorming and collaboration, the employees had come up with a list of about 10 customer-focused initiatives as part of a broader strategy. The marketing director and the whole team were happy with the result. I shared their enthusiasm. They were all worthwhile projects. I was about to congratulate them on their work and say goodbye, when I suddenly felt a sense of doubt amongst the group.

'Steven,' someone said, '*it was a lot of fun and we are confident about these projects, but we think our CEO will block them.*' I was a bit shocked as I had discussed the project plans with the CEO and had the impression that he was positive about the whole thing.

'*That's a nasty feeling,*' I responded, '*what do you propose?*'
'*Would you be willing to present our 10 initiatives to our CEO? He might be more open to the ideas if they come from you.*'
'*This is new to me, but I would certainly be happy to give it a try.*'

A few minutes later, I was on the second floor of the building, sitting in the office of their CEO, a very pleasant and friendly man. I introduced the various projects to him; he was excited by them, and he immediately approved all but one that did not appeal to him. '*We should have done some of these things a long time ago,*' he said exuberantly at one point. I returned to the workshop room and, full of confidence, gave the group the good news. But they thought my message was not convincing enough and said, '*We want to hear it directly from our CEO!*' I went back upstairs and this time I returned with the CEO who found the situation rather strange.

With just as much enthusiasm as the first time, he approved the projects one by one. I felt good. It seemed that the issue of trust had been resolved. But just when everyone seemed 80% convinced that the projects were safe, the CEO's voice echoed across the room: 'You have my agreement to do all those things but remember that ultimately it is the sales figures that determine whether we have done a good job or not. So don't forget to put most of your time into selling products. But mind you, I really do support these nine initiatives.' **The CEO left and the energy disappeared from the room.**

ARE YOU A CUSTOMER-CENTRIC LEADER?

Everyone in that room had realised what had just happened, except for the CEO. His feeling was: I gave the necessary support and ended with a slight nuance to the whole story. It is these little phrases or decisions that make or break credibility. Those little slips of the tongue often reveal certain ideas or fixed patterns of thinking that exist in a company. It is not always easy to work on these. This is why I have developed three qualitative questions. The answers reveal if a person is a customer-centric leader.

There are various ways to gauge a company's customer-centricity. You can use the Net Promoter Score (NPS) which gauges enthusiasm, loyalty and satisfaction with a company,[40] or use customer feedback. Both are informative. However, my experience has shown that the answers to these three qualitative questions will teach you more about the presence or lack of customer-oriented culture within an organisation, as well as the credibility of the company's leader(s) in this domain.

Opposing interests?

Fix it? Or who did it?

How empowered is your front line staff?

1. What do you decide when there are conflicting interests: what if the interests of your company and those of your customer do not coincide? How do you react?
2. Do you solve the problem or start an investigation first? Do you always opt for the client's solution, or do you want to know all the details of the case first?
3. How much responsibility do you delegate to your employees for keeping customers happy? How far are they allowed to go before they have to ask the boss's permission?

Let us look at these qualitative questions in real life scenarios:

QUESTION 1. WHAT DO YOU IF THERE IS A CONFLICT OF INTEREST BETWEEN YOUR COMPANY AND THE CUSTOMER?

Dormant accounts are common in the telecom sector. They might belong to customers with for example a SIM card in an old iPad that is no longer being used. Sometimes the customer has lost track of this and continues to pay a monthly fee for the SIM card. Telecom companies know perfectly well which customers are paying for dormant accounts; that information is readily available to them.

What options does a company have for dealing with this?
– Do nothing. Just let these accounts lie dormant. After all, the customer has not cancelled their contract and you are not doing anything wrong. So why not let sleeping dogs lie and retain the revenue?
– Act proactively. Call the owners of the dormant accounts and ask them what they wish to do with their subscription. This allows the customer to choose what is best for them.
– Refund them. Call the owners of the dormant accounts and pay them back for the undelivered value. After all, these customers paid each month for something they did not use and often had forgotten about; like going to the bakery every week, paying for a loaf of bread, but leaving the loaf behind in the shop.

You can feel the difference in the three responses to one of my qualitative questions. They range from not customer-centric at all to extremely customer-centric. Every telecom company I have worked with has dormant accounts; each has a 'we want to be very customer-centric' slide in its corporate presentation; and every one of them just lets those accounts sleep. How do you react when there are conflicting interests? Your behaviour and decisions around these kinds of issues determines if your employees will believe that you want to be customer-centric. **The essential question is very simple: are you willing to hurt yourself in the short term to gain trust in the long term?** If the answer to this question is 'no', then you will never be able to build a true customer-centric culture.

By now you may be thinking: but Steven, nobody does that, right?
There are companies that do dare to take decisions that cost them money in the short term but help them build trust in the long term. In-N-Out Burger, the very popular US burger chain, is such an example. This fast-food chain was started in 1948 by Harry and Esther Snyder in Baldwin Park, southern California.[41] As of 2023, there are 387 In-N-Out Burger restaurants across the United States, with 267 of these located in California. **If you go to the company's website, or you eat at one of their outlets, you will not notice anything special at first glance.** They sell burgers, fries and milkshakes like any burger restaurant does. And yet, In-N-Out Burger has, for years, ranked first in its industry for customer satisfaction. Eighty percent of In-N-Out Burger customers say they are satisfied or very satisfied, compared with only 40% at McDonald's or Burger King.[42]

That is correct, a two-fold difference! And this has led to some crazy scenes. In-N-Out opened its first restaurant in the state of Colorado in 2020. The hype was so great that there were mile-long queues to enter the restaurant. At one point, customers were waiting up to 12 hours![43] The local police had to use social media to call for people to stop going to the burger joint, because traffic in that region was completely gridlocked. How crazy is that? In other words, someone could have flown from Denver, Colorado to San Francisco, lunched at an In-N-Out there, flown back to Denver and have taken less to do this than if they had stood in that queue.

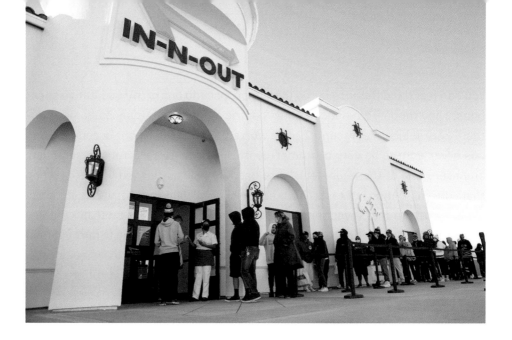

So, what is behind this? After all, this commotion was over cheeseburgers and not the latest technological gadget or the newest Harry Potter attraction.

Ever since In-N-Out was founded, they have always been 100% committed to top-quality products and a fun, pleasant atmosphere. For example, they have deliberately chosen not to start a franchise model or go public with the company. They want to keep everything in their own hands and always be able to make the best choice for the customer.[44] Zero compromises are made. For example, they decided to close all their 37 restaurants in Texas for two days because of a bun mishap. Their explanation for the closures: *'At In-N-Out Burgers, we have always served the highest quality food with no compromise. We recently discovered that our buns in Texas do not meet the quality standards that we demand. There was and are no food safety concerns. We decided to close all of our Texas stores until we are confident that we can serve our normal high-quality bun.'[45]* This is how they proved to customers that they do not compromise. This is how to build a fan base willing to queue for 12 hours – by showing year after year that you do not compromise on customer focus. Oh, and lest you think profitability and money are not important at this company: the profitability of an In-N-Out Burger restaurant is about double (!) the profitability of a McDonald's restaurant.[46]

Closing those restaurants not only makes customers happy, it also makes your employees realise where your priority lies. With the customer!

Are you willing to hurt yourself in the short term in return for earning the trust of your customers in the long term?

QUESTION 2. WHAT DO YOU DO FIRST?
SOLVE THE PROBLEM OR START AN INVESTIGATION?

Mistakes happen. The important point is how we deal with them. It is now accepted that customer satisfaction can be higher after a mistake, if it is solved properly, than if a mistake never occurred. Yet this turns out to be even more complicated in practice than in theory.

There are two options in the case of a mistake. Solve the problem immediately or first investigate exactly what happened and who is responsible for the error. It is my experience that, increasingly, companies choose the second option. It appears the thinking is, 'First let's find out what went wrong and second find out whether it was us or the customer that caused this error.' Meanwhile, time is lost, and the customer becomes nervous. After a few days there is usually an unpleasant exchange of messages: 'Dear customer, we have seen that the fault does not actually lie with us, but...' In most cases, this sentence will lead to a negative reaction: 'Okay, maybe it is indeed (partly) my fault, but I have been a customer of your company for more than 10 years! Despite this, you are unwilling to help me!' Most companies eventually decided to solve the problem to maintain the customer relationship. But this results in frustration for the customer and the company with no one truly happy about how things turned out.

There are two options for responding to a mistake: (i) you can immediately do everything possible to solve the problem. Even if the responsibility lies (partly) with the customer, you can put your own ego aside and help your customer. By doing this, you will have a satisfied customer. **Or (ii) take an opportunity to learn from the mistake.** Discuss with the customer how the mistake could have happened and how both parties can ensure that it will not happen again. This discussion will be more constructive than the first option (i). In both cases, you help the customer, but only the second approach leads to the result that everyone is satisfied as well.

My advice is to use a hybrid of the two options. Fix the errors immediately if possible and only then analyse what went wrong and speak with the customer. Sometimes I meet with resistance when I recommend this approach. 'Steven, you don't know our customers: some of them are slobs.' In other words, sometimes our clients abuse our kindness, and we suffer. I fully understand that feeling. That kind of customer does exist. In my previous book *The Offer You Can't Refuse*', I called it the 95%/5% rule in customer experience and wrote about this in Chapter 2 of the present book. It bears repeating. Five percent of customers will drain you dry, but 95% of them are normal, decent people. People tend to think and talk too much about that five percent of people, to the point that we think of them as the average customer. But they are not. That is an error of our brains. The moment you recognise that 95% of people are normal and decent you will start offering truly customer-centric services.

Smartphoto is one of the largest photo production websites in Europe. They offer printing services, create photo books and print your photos on all kinds of objects. During a brainstorm with the team, someone had the idea of launching a new service. *'What if we offer our customers a new photo book for free if the customer makes a mistake in their photo book!'* Like with most brainstorms, half the participants were excited by the idea and the other half did not like it. *'It's a good idea, but make no mistake, some customers are going to abuse it! They will deliberately make a small typo somewhere in their photo book to get two photo books for the price of one. So, they and the couple they travelled with will get a photo book for half the price.'*

After an intense discussion, CEO Stef De corte decided to just give it a try. Six months after initiating the programme, they had mailed off only a handful of photo books for free. Customers apparently do their best to make their photo books as perfect as possible. Even if someone does deliberately make an error to get a second photo book for free, the small cost does not outweigh the extra trust customers gain in Smartphoto. They accept that five percent of customers may deliberately abuse the offer but target the other 95%. One way to view Smartphoto's offer is that it solves the issue of mistakes in advance. No discussion needed. Moreover, the staff saw Stef's reaction in that debate. He took the side of the customer without any compromise. That way, you get satisfied customers and employees believe you really mean it when you say that you want to be customer oriented.

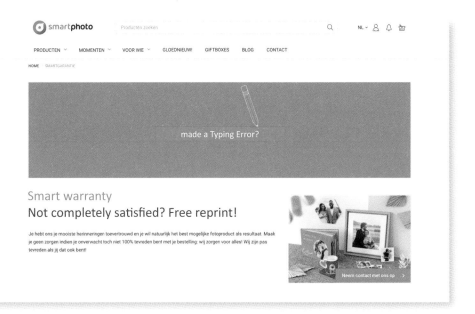

smartphoto

PRODUCTEN ⌄   MOMENTEN ⌄   VOOR WIE ⌄   GLOEDNIEUW!   GIFTBOXES   BLOG   CONTACT

HOME   SMARTGARANTIE

made a Typing Error?

Smart warranty
Not completely satisfied? Free reprint!

Je hebt ons je mooiste herinneringen toevertrouwd en je wil natuurlijk het best mogelijke fotoproduct als resultaat. Maak je geen zorgen indien je onverwacht toch niet 100% tevreden bent met je bestelling: wij zorgen voor alles! Wij zijn pas tevreden als jij dat ook bent!

Neem contact met ons op   ❯

QUESTION 3: HOW MUCH RESPONSIBILITY DO YOUR EMPLOYEES HAVE TO MAKE DECISIONS?

If you really want to get customers excited, you must have help from the people closest to them. Employees from the customer service team, salespeople, and so forth see and hear customers every day. These employees are important touchpoints in your customer experience. Do these people have the freedom and authority to make their own decisions when discussing and solving incidents with customers?

One thing a customer does not want to hear is: 'I'm not allowed to make that decision; I have to ask the manager.' This is your tip that you are heading for a difficult discussion. **What customers want is very simple: to be helped immediately or to get an answer to their question immediately. To succeed in this, it is important to delegate as much responsibility as possible to the employees.**

One of the best examples of this is a policy at the Ritz-Carlton hotel group. This luxury brand has one of the most beautiful marketing slogans I have heard. 'We are ladies and gentlemen serving ladies and gentlemen.' Very nicely put! The Ritz-Carlton has a famous '$2,000 Rule'. Each employee has the authority to compensate and surprise customers up to an amount of USD 2,000. Imagine you have booked a nice room in one of their hotels. Upon entering your room, you find soiled towels, from a previous guest, lying on the bathroom floor. Of course, this is not what you expected, so you immediately call housekeeping. The person that answers your call has the responsibility to fix the problem and make sure the customer is happy with the result. They will say something like, 'Our apologies! We will send someone to the room immediately to resolve that. Meanwhile, you and your partner are invited to relax in our bar and you will find two glasses of champagne waiting for you there. When you return to your room, you will find it in perfect order. Have a nice day!' The employee solves the problem and immediately provides compensation, without the need to consult a manager. This instant response gives a good feeling to the customer but also to the employee who is happy that they were able to help a customer.[47]

" We are ladies and gentlemen serving ladies and gentlemen "

THE RITZ-CARLTON

The $2000 Rule goes beyond providing compensation when a problem arises. Management also encourages employees to look for opportunities to surprise people positively even if something has not gone wrong. The encouragement sounds like this: *'Use your time, your energy and – if necessary – the company's money to give customers an unforgettable experience.'*

Many business leaders do not dare to adopt such policies, fearing that employees cannot handle the responsibility. This is where the 95%/5% rule applies to employees. Five percent of your employees are bound to misuse the rule, but the vast majority want to do well and are perfectly capable of using their common sense. If you do not trust your own employees, you may have a problem with your hiring strategy.

Of course, it is not the case that the staff at the Ritz-Carlton give expensive gifts to people all the time for no reason. However, I experienced the top quality of this service personally when a few years ago a client asked me to give a lecture at the Ritz-Carlton Hotel in Key Biscayne near Miami, Florida. Upon arrival at the hotel, I realised that I had failed to bring my iPhone charger. I did not have enough time to dash to a shop to buy a replacement. I explained my predicament to a member of staff who engaged the hotel team to come to my rescue; **'No problem, Mr Van Belleghem, we will solve your problem.** The solution was not, **'You can charge your phone using one of our chargers and come and pick it up in an hour.'** No, instead someone was sent off to buy a new charger. An hour later, I was notified that I could pick it up from the concierge. *On the house!* That was the $2,000 Rule in action, and I can only confirm that, as a customer, it felt like top-notch service.

People sometimes ask, 'Why does the Ritz-Carlton put a limit on that amount? Why don't they instruct the staff to help the customer, whatever it takes, whatever the cost is. There is a rational and an emotional reason for this. The rational reason is the *life-time value* of the Ritz's clients. That amounts to $250,000 per client. From that perspective, USD 2,000 is not an excessive amount to engender brand loyalty.

The emotional reason has to do with the mental comfort of employees. Chances are if you were to ask employees to, *'Help customers and do what is needed: price doesn't matter'*, they will not believe you. Defining an explicit amount provides a kind of mental comfort. You can compare it to the demarcation of the swimming area in the sea. Thanks to those clear boundaries, swimmers dare to swim to the end of the safe zone. If those boundaries were not there, chances are that many people would not dare to swim that far.

MAKE THEM BELIEVE

The above three questions are a kind of mirror for yourself to see how customer-focused you really are. A self-assessment, using your responses to these questions, can explain why you succeed or fail in building a strong customer culture. The answer to these three questions provides insight into whether your team will or will not believe that you are, or wish to become, customer focused.

Think about how words and actions can be balanced. You say your call centre is important, but how many days a year will you sit in one of your call centre's chairs? If a busy weekend is expected in your shops, would it not be a good idea to help in one of your shops on that weekend? **There are several simple actions that you can incorporate into the way you work and into your overall leadership style that will increase the credibility of your focus on the customer experience.**

◆ **A positive flow**

Try to make the most of every opportunity to share positive customer stories. Not all customer experience feedback needs to be in the form of an official message. If an email arrives with positive feedback, or a customer says something nice to a co-worker, or you see a positive review on social media... all of these can be shared with the rest of the team concerned and the whole company. A flow of positivity from customers helps generate a sense of pride amongst all your employees. By drawing attention to that positive feedback, your employees also notice how important it is to you.

◆ **Have their backs**

One of the friendliest pursers I have ever come across was on a flight I took from Frankfurt to Oslo. I felt so sorry for the poor guy. He apologised for four (!) different situations during that short flight. Sorry that we left late. Sorry that the luggage compartment is so full that you must fly with things on your lap. Sorry for not having any information on connecting flights. Sorry that you must deboard through the middle door of the plane instead of the front.

I wondered how someone who had to deliver so much negative news could be kept motivated. So much went wrong on that flight and there was no support from the purser's colleagues. He was on his own and things were not going well. Such powerlessness and perhaps frustration does not feel good, especially for someone who is so intrinsically motivated. Powerlessness erodes motivation. As a leader, it is important to support people, to find ways that you can help them do their job better. Things will go wrong from time to time, but if employees feel supported when things go wrong, their level of motivation will rise.

◆ Where is the party?

You do not have to try hard to find reasons to motivate your employees. Fifty-eight percent of company employees say that regular positive feedback and appreciation, a simple 'Thank you!', 'Well done!', or 'Great job!' has a very positive impact on their morale.[48] Giving credit occasionally to an employee who has done something customer-focused also demonstrates the importance of the customer experience to the management and the company. For instance, KeyBank, a regional US bank, launched a programme in which employees could give each other 'Key Kudos' for a good customer-focused action. At San Francisco airport, KeyBank's team has a 'you are one of a kind' philosophy. Those who are exceptionally kind to customers can be honoured through this programme. Actions that are celebrated in a company are seen as something important by employees. Celebrate your customer experience successes and it rises in importance.

◆ Micro decisions

Micro decisions are of paramount importance to the theme of this chapter: how small things we do or don't say and do have a huge effect on our credibility and on the ability of those around us, and especially those we lead, to believe in us. Think for a moment about seemingly unimportant situations where our credibility is judged. If an employee has done something exceptional for a customer, but at a price a bit more than you would like, how do you respond? Do you say, 'A super initiative. I'm glad that the customer is happy.' Or do you say, 'Well done, but fortunately we don't have that cost with every customer.' What part of the latter response will the employee remember?

The team leader thinks they have complimented the employee and the employee thinks they have been warned not to repeat this gesture to any customers again. It is the little things that determine the future behaviour of your team members.

◆ Do you have a Mr Wolf?

When Marsellus Wallace from the cast of *Pulp Fiction* had problems, who did he call? Right! Mr Wolf, a 'cleaner' who cleaned up difficult problems. Every now and then you need someone like Mr Wolf to push through your customer experience strategy. A person you can rely on 100% who has the necessary decisiveness, authority and common sense to help you sort things out. As Churchill said, 'There is no problem so complex, there is no crisis so big that it cannot be solved within 20 minutes.' Sometimes you need decisiveness instead of endless deliberation. That's when you call in your very own Mr Wolf.

IT IS NOT ABOUT MEASURING YOUR SUCCESS; IT IS ABOUT BUILDING A CULTURE

If you invest in a customer culture, you will obviously want to measure the success of your efforts. I am indifferent about the tool that you use. Whether it measured through a customer satisfaction survey or NPS or another tool is irrelevant. The important thing is what you do with the outcome.

Too many companies massage customer satisfaction data. An obsession with numbers is not a good thing. A good NPS or satisfaction score results from a strong customer culture. Not the other way around! Customer focus does not begin with a target number in your annual report. It starts with your company's mindset and actions. The result is a good figure.

If you purely use numbers and data to make decisions, chances are you will make the wrong decisions. From time to time, it helps to remind yourself about what lies at the core of your business. Then ask yourself what you want your business to achieve. When 16-year-old Harry Styles auditioned for The X Factor in 2010, things did not get off to a good start. He sang off beat and out of tune. Usually that would mean game over. But Simon Cowell, of course, was one of the judges. Many X Factor candidates are afraid of him, but he has a track record of discovering talent. He finds rough diamonds time and time again. At about 30 seconds into his audition, Cowell asked Styles to stop singing. The audience thought he intended to end Styles' embarrassing display. Instead, Cowell asked Styles to sing without musical accompaniment because he felt the music distracted him from hearing Styles' voice. Styles chose to sing Stevie Wonder's song *Isn't She Lovely*.

It was time for the judges to cast their votes on whether Styles should continue in the competition. Cowell was immediately convinced, but his fellow judge, Robert Rinder, was not, saying, *'Harry, you are not experienced enough and not ready for this. For all those good reasons, I vote "no".* Cowell stared wide-eyed at Rinder. He seemed to be thinking, 'How can this guy not appreciate this boy's talent?' And he might have said, *'Robert, sometimes you must go back to the core. Why did we start this programme? To discover rough diamonds and with the right guidance grow them into great talents and stars. Right,'* was Cowell's rejoinder. In the end, most judges voted 'yes' and Harry Styles went on to become a superstar.

Why was our company founded? Why do we exist? How do we get customers excited? Often the answer is very simple, found without using an Excel spreadsheet. Look at the most logical solution without considering the complex structure of a company. Look through the data and decide what is the right thing to do, just as it was the right thing to do to give Harry Styles another chance. Look through the facts and trust your common sense in doing so.

Do not get me wrong. I am big believer in measuring the results of your efforts. There is no doubt about that. It's just that you must plan and execute your efforts in the right way and in the right order or there will be consequences.

'MAKE YOUR BED!'

On 17 May 2014, Admiral William H. McRaven gave an impressive speech to the graduates of the University of Texas at Austin.[49] At the time, William McRaven had been a US Navy SEAL, a special operations force within the US Navy, for 36 years. The training programme for this elite group of soldiers is demanding. It involves six long and tough months of running long distances in soft sand and swimming at midnight in the cold waters of the Atlantic Ocean and other physically and mentally draining activities. During the process, professionally trained warriors weed out candidates who are physically or mentally weak to prevent them from becoming a Navy SEAL. During his speech, McRaven summarised 10 important life lessons from his time of training to become a SEAL.

McRaven's first life lesson was, for me, the most telling and applies perfectly to building a customer culture with your team. Every morning during SEAL training, the instructors, all Vietnam War veterans during McRaven's time in training, would enter the candidates' barracks. They began their inspection with the candidates' beds. The sheet and blanket of a properly made bed were to be tightly stretched and folded at the corners to form a sharp triangle and the pillow was to be fluffed up and placed in the middle of the bed. It was easily the simplest task of the day, but a perfectly made bed was expected every day during training.

'If you made your bed properly in the morning, you had successfully completed the first assignment of the day. It gave you a small sense of pride and it motivated you to finish the next assignment equally well,' explained McRaven, a note of determination in his voice.

Then came the most important message from his life lesson: 'If you can't do the little things right, you will never do the big things right!'

If you would like your team to believe that customer-centricity is important to you, then you should not only focus on big and strategic projects, but rather look for the little things that can be done better. If you do some small things very well every day and highlight them, the team will understand what is important to you and important for the company. Likewise, it is the details of a customer relationship that can make the difference. When building a customer culture, it is better to invest in 100 small projects that you can do very well, rather than to try and tackle two or three big strategic projects that take months of work.

YOU NEED ACTION!
THE *HOW TO BECOME A SHINY DIAMOND* WORKBOOK

You need to take action to build belief within your company! Action results from concrete, easy-to-understand, small and clearly defined steps. I remember when Belgian telecoms player, Telenet, began to optimise their customer journeys at a very concrete point: customer relocation. Telenet had received many complaints about that process, and it was a clearly defined problem. After optimising that process, the positive feedback came, giving energy to move on to the next customer journey, and so on.

If your company is planning a transformation to become more customer-centric, it is a good idea to start with some kind of launch campaign. This will make your intentions clear to everyone. I recommend that companies organise a 'Four-week shiny diamond challenge'. During that challenge, you tackle small steps to become customer-centric. The first challenge can be a kind of kick-off campaign. Then you review the results and start the next challenge.

If you want to build a customer culture, you need actions to support your credibility. For example, stage a monthly challenge. Even try to encourage people to do something small every day.

To motivate yourself and your team to implement these actions consistently, I have also created a 'How to become a shiny diamond workbook'. This action-oriented workbook motivates you to keep up your daily customer efforts.

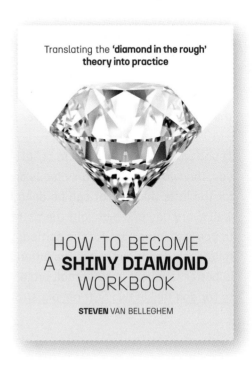

Translating the **'diamond in the rough' theory into practice**

HOW TO BECOME
A **SHINY DIAMOND**
WORKBOOK

STEVEN VAN BELLEGHEM

The workbook guides you to:

- ◆ Score yourself on the different aspects of the shiny diamond.
- ◆ Initiate and follow up on the 'Four-week shiny diamond challenges'.
- ◆ Spend 10 minutes a week sorting out your thoughts to make the process move forward much faster. 10 minutes a week. That is all I ask.
- ◆ Record positive feedback you received from a particular client.
- ◆ Record what you have learned each week.
- ◆ Decide what action you will take based on what you learned that week.
- ◆ Choose which strategic projects you need to transform your company into a polished diamond.

Writing these things down, reflecting on them and keeping track of them, will force you to take more actions and in a sustainable way.

If you are interested in getting started with the 'How to become a shiny diamond workbook', check out www.stevenvanbelleghem.com/diamond. You can download the digital version of the workbook for free and you can purchase hard copies.

THE ROUGH DIAMOND
VERSUS THE BRIGHT DIAMOND

We have reached the end of the second part, where the aim was to transform our rough diamond into a bright diamond. A bright diamond is a company where all stakeholders (the board, management, investors, employees, customers) are convinced (Believe!) about the importance of creating impact in a positive way (the TOP GUN effect) for customers and for society (The circle of influence). A bright diamond is the foundation for making customer culture come alive.

Here are the 13 differences between a Rough Diamond and a Bright Diamond:

	Rough Diamond	Bright Diamond
1	Complaining, negative mindset	Positive mindset
2	Focus on the problems	Focus on the opportunities
3	Only interested in own business	Wants to make the world a bit better
4	Dares not share opinion on society	Is a clear voice in public debate
5	Customer Experience is nice to have	Customer Experience is central
6	Micro decisions demotivate	Micro decisions support (CX)
7	CX is too complex and theoretical	CX is action-oriented
8	Only sales results are celebrated	Sales results and CX are celebrated
9	Only focus on customer data	Focus on data and customer, gut feeling
10	Long and slow feedback loop	(Almost) real time feedback loops
11	Not willing to suffer short-term pain	Pain over costs is OK if it builds trust
12	Investigation first when there is an error	First fix error, then investigation
13	Employees ask permission to do something for customer	Employees are encouraged to do the right things for customers them-selves

Perhaps you could bring these concepts to life in your own organisation. Suppose you had to score yourself on a 10-point scale for each of these 13 points. In doing so, we remove the 5 from the scale to eliminate a neutral response. On which of these items do you score in the upper half of the scale, and for which do you score in the lower half of the scale? Where do you have the greatest distinction and where do you fail badly?

Perhaps you could share this table at a team meeting and ask your fellow executives or your team members to score your company on these dimensions. That will give you a very good idea of how bright your diamond is today. It will also help you evaluate which of these dimensions you can improve on to make the diamond even brighter than it already is today.

CONCRETE CUSTOMER EXPERIENCE TIPS FROM THIS CHAPTER:

1. Have your own way of communicating analysed. Where do you motivate or demotivate employees to be customer-centric. Learn to understand your own communication better to become a better leader.

2. Practise saying certain motivational phrases when employees have done something special for a customer, even if it took a bit more time and money than you may have liked. While doing so, restrain yourself from correcting them.

3. If you organise a brainstorm or workshop on the customer experience, make it only about the customer experience. Exclude all other topics from the agenda. Focus!

4. Dare to be on the side of the customer when there is an opposing interest and communicate this to your team. 'We accept short-term pain in order to win trust in the long term.'

5. Do not make customers pay for something that gives them no value.

6. If a mistake happens or there is a problem: solve it. Do not begin analysing what went wrong until you have solved the problem.

7. Believe in the 95%-5% rule and make decisions for the 95% 'normal' customers.

8. Trust your team. Give them the necessary tools to make customers happy and give them the freedom to choose the best solution themselves.

9. Inspire your team with 'random acts of kindness' that you yourself have organised for customers. Invite them to do the same.

10. If something has gone wrong between an employee and a customer, the leader's job is to help the customer and support the employee.

11. Every week, share any positive messages you have received from a customer.

12. Work with a customer's 'quote of the week'.

13. If someone has done something exceptional to help a customer, praise that employee (literally).

14. Look for small frictions in your customer relationship every month and resolve them every month. Involve employees in this process.
15. Organise a 'customer challenge' with your team every month. 'What are we going to do this month to make customers extra happy?'
16. Start every meeting with a positive story from a customer.
17. At Christmas, give your employees a budget of 50 Euro with which they can make customers happy. Only condition: it should be a personalised gift or surprise so that the customer feels you tried.
18. Start complimenting each other every day. 'You handled this very well yesterday towards that customer.'
19. When someone becomes a customer, what little gift can you give them to make them feel good right away?
20. Think for a moment how you can greet customers via mail, phone, face to face to make them feel good. What do you personally like and how can you use that in your industry?
21. Promise only what you can deliver. Organise your own success: promise something with a margin that allows you to deliver faster than promised.
22. Think about 'the power of moments'. What aspect in the customer journey creates an initial peak in the relationship and how can you end with a peak at the end of the customer journey?
23. When Marsellus Wallace in *Pulp Fiction* had problems, he would call Mr Wolf, a 'cleaner' who would come and clean up the difficult problems. Who is your Mr Wolf? Who has the decisiveness and authority to sort out customer experience challenges with a good dose of common sense? Every company needs someone like that.
24. Train your leaders to make them aware of the impact of their micro-communications and micro-decisions. Employees watch their behaviour much more than they value their words.
25. Ensure psychological safety in your team. If something goes wrong, do not start blaming but just deal with it in a very analytical way: what went wrong and how can we avoid it in the future?

THE POLISHED DIAMOND

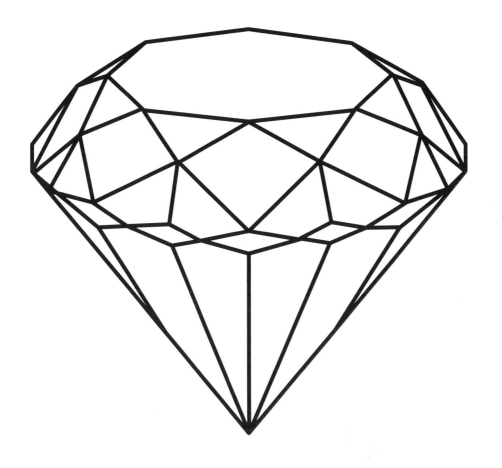

PART 2: THE POLISHED DIAMOND

Now that we have a beautiful, bright diamond, it's time to cut and polish it. We turn it into a beautiful, stunning jewel that most people would be happy to wear.

The bright diamond makes it bright to everyone what their ambition is; the cut and polished diamond also fulfils that ambition. First and foremost, the bright diamond ensures that internally everyone clearly understands what the objective is. The cut and polished diamond shows customers how nice it is to be a customer of your company. The attitude and actions to achieve a cut diamond builds the customer culture that every customer dreams of.

This section covers three aspects to transform the diamond into a polished jewel.

How to really prove to the customer that you are loyal to her/him (Chapter 5)
We often ask the wrong question: How can we make our customers more loyal? It is the other way around. How can we prove our loyalty to the customer? If we show our loyalty to the customer first, we will eventually be rewarded with their trust, and their loyalty. Building loyalty starts with the company; the customer follows.

How to build the right customer culture (Chapter 6)
How do we ensure that we continuously improve our understanding of our customers over time? And how can we put that knowledge into practice in a proactive and organised way? If we get this right, we will ultimately succeed in becoming a partner in our customers' lives.

How can technology help us polish off all the rough edges? (Chapter 7)
It has become very difficult to build a top customer experience without good technology. On the other hand, technology is not a short-cut to making customers happy. In what ways can we use technology in collaboration with our human employees in the most impactful way possible to really make the diamond shine?

CHAPTER 5

THE CUSTOMER LOYALTY FLYWHEEL

'WE'RE WITH YOU **WHATEVER HAPPENS'**

HERMIONE GRANGER

WHAT IF FRIENDS BECOME CUSTOMERS?

Most entrepreneurs are busy helping their customers every day. After a while, serving customers becomes routine. You perform your work without giving it much thought. Bakers prepare almost the same loaves and pastries every day. Roofers repair a roof every day or lay a new roof. Surgeons perform the same operation for the 500th time. Most people's work eventually becomes routine. Routine means that you stop thinking about how you do your job; the task is carried out automatically by your body. Even interactions with customers become routine. You are asked the same questions every day and you know how to best respond and what not to say. Routines create a certain mental calm and can also ensure a good standard of service.

But what if you suddenly receive a request from one of your best friends. 'Say, we have decided to renovate our house. Would you be free to lead the project for us?' At that moment, your routine response stops. When friends become clients, your emotional response is different from when you are asked to lead a project at work. **When friends become clients, you want the project to go as well as possible. After all, a lot depends on it. This is no longer just about a customer relationship; this is about a friendship.** This is about avoiding years of jokes at parties should you mess up the job. When friends become clients, you work long hours to make sure you deliver on your promise. That energy and desire to do extra well, like when friends become clients, is an energy every client should feel from you. This is the only way to build long-term customer loyalty. This is not to imply that customers should become friends. My message is that customers want to feel that unique energy and determination emanating from you to do right by them.

SHOW UP WITH PASSION!

What is routine for you is not routine at all for your customers. Most people remodel only once in a couple of decades. For them, remodelling causes stress. Acknowledging the presence of stress will get the customer relationship off to a good start. For many people, buying a new car is a fun experience. For the salesperson, it is their daily routine. If a salesperson does not sense and share in the customer's enthusiasm, the customer will be disappointed. The highlight of their week would become a mediocre moment. The potentially shining diamond will remain rough. A car salesman can do their job well but still fail to elicit and respond to positive emotion from their customers. If you ask customers for feedback, they might rate the interaction as positive overall. However, a positive score is not enough to win their loyalty.

Forrester, a customer experience consultancy, studied behaviour and actions that engender brand loyalty. The study revealed that positive emotions create loyalty and strong bonds between customers and brands.[50] A car salesman who knows how to mirror the customer's enthusiasm and is also able to share the customer's pleasure over a new model or an exciting option can get customers excited. **The art of breaking one's own routine and going along with the customer's positive emotions is a behaviour that will build loyalty.**

In September 2022, I had the pleasure of speaking at the influential Oslo Business Forum. Felipe Gomez was one of the other speakers. Felipe is from Colombia, where he built a great career in several large Colombian companies. His real passion, however, is music and he is a talented pianist. At one point, he decided to find out for himself what qualities are needed to become a good pianist. His conclusion was that the same skills are needed to be a success as a pianist or as a businessperson. Arguably, they are also the same skills needed for a successful career in sports. Felipe has developed a brilliant keynote presentation in which he presents insights from the combination of music and management. A central theme of Felipe's message was 'show up with passion'. He played a beautiful classical piece by Bach during his presentation. The first time, he played it perfectly technically, but without feeling. It sounded good and there was absolutely nothing wrong with it, but there was no lump in my throat, no frisson. Felipe played it a second time, with love and passion. The difference was impressive. The music sounded richer and more emotional. The difference between doing your job well and doing your job with passion is not something visible. It is something the customer feels.

MY MOST UNIQUE DINNER EVER!

I was out with colleagues for a special celebratory dinner. We had reservations at Nuance, a two-star Michelin restaurant. We arrived at the restaurant full of curiosity and enthusiasm, but there was a problem. We were there on Friday night, September 5th, but we had made a mistake and booked for the 5th December! Sofie, the restaurant's hostess, panicked for a moment. *'Our restaurant is fully booked this evening and there are eight of you,'* she said, her voice full of regret. Our group stood awkwardly at the reception desk, not knowing what to say, when Sofie said, *'I have an idea. Why don't you go to the café across street and have a drink on their terrace. I'll get back to you in 15 minutes.'*

We enjoyed a quiet aperitif on the terrace across the street. It was a beautiful evening. Fifteen minutes later, Sofie appeared and said, with a beaming smile **'Follow me, please.'** Our curiosity grew as we followed her back across the street, through Nuance's entrance, across the dining room, and through an exit and emerged onto a small courtyard. There stood a beautifully set table with at least 20 candles on it. *'Is it ok if you sit here this evening? The chef will serve you personally. Because space is limited, we will need to place the bottles of wine directly on the table, rather than in wine*

bucket stands. Will this suit you?' We were hugely impressed by the excellent solution Sophie had found for us. It was a fantastic evening and one of my best experiences ever as a customer.

At the end of the evening, one of my colleagues asked, *'What would you have done if it had been raining?'*
'I would have put you in our private dining room upstairs,' Sophie replied. *'Letting you go home without a meal was not an option.'*

It would have been so easy for Sofie to simply apologise for not having room for us and then send us packing. After all, we had made the booking error; it was not the restaurant's fault. **But her passion for her work took over: she wanted us to have a lovely evening and, together with her husband, who it transpired was the chef, did everything possible to make it happen. Passion and a sincere desire to help people form the bedrock of eternal customer loyalty.**

LOYALTY TO THE BRAND OR TO A LOYALTY PROGRAMME

Companies have been asking themselves the wrong question for years: 'What should we do to make our customers more loyal to our brand?' This is the wrong question. In fact, we should turn that question around and ask ourselves, 'What can we do to show our loyalty to the customer?'

Customer loyalty does not start with the customer. First, as a company, you prove your loyalty to the customer and only then does the customer follow. Marketing theory frequently describes customer loyalty as a sentiment that begins with the customer. This implies that when the customer does their utmost, we will reciprocate. This standard is biased against the development of loyalty by the Never Normal customer, who is opinionated, outspoken and demanding, and has a low exit cost. (Read more about the Never Normal customer in Chapter 9).

The best (or worst) examples of this are airline loyalty programmes. Because I regularly travel internationally on business, I am a platinum or golden member of several mileage award programmes. Some of these frequent flyer programmes are shared by multiple airlines. I appreciate the benefits these programmes provide, such as faster check-in, a fast lane at security and occasional free upgrades. These are all nice things. Yet I ask myself sometimes if these perks encourage me to be loyal to an airline or programme. In my case, the answer is the latter. I like having the benefits of being a frequent flyer, but the airline I fly with is unimportant to me. The efficiency of the route is much more important to me than the brand painted on the tail of the plane.

Occasionally the benefits of being a frequent flyer strike me as wrong . I was in Berlin one day, booked to return to Amsterdam with KLM. I arrived at the airport much earlier than scheduled, which meant I could potentially catch an earlier flight home. My flight was scheduled for 6pm, but at around 4pm another KLM flight would depart for Amsterdam. I asked the staff at check-in if there was a seat available on the earlier flight so I could be back home a bit earlier. The immediate answer was negative. 'No, unfortunately that's not possible, sir. Our apologies.' Then I did something I do not really like to do and said, *'Madam, I am a platinum customer with KLM. Is there really no possibility of a seat on the earlier flight?'* The word platinum changed everything. A few taps on the computer and I was given a new boarding card for a seat that had suddenly become available. At that moment, a woman approached check-in with the same request. She, too, got 'no' as an answer and left, looking disappointed. The employee winked at me and said, *'We do this only for our platinum customers.'* I boarded the plane and found that about 20% of the seats were empty. I felt embarrassed. KLM apparently believes the selective treatment of passengers in such situations increases customer loyalty, but for me, it had the opposite effect. I felt so bad that the other passenger was not allowed to board the flight. Customer loyalty should start with the company, not the customer. In any case, the customer loyalty of the woman who was denied the option to change her flight will not have improved and neither did mine.

Loyalty programmes miss the mark when managed this way. Loyalty to a programme may be valuable in the short term, but in the long term, you are not actually building value for your business.

WILD ALASKAN COMPANY PROVES ITS LOYALTY

The Wild Alaskan Company is a seafood delivery company in the United States. It was founded in 2017 by Arron Kallenberg. Arron was born and raised in Alaska. He spent most of his childhood on his parents' fishing boat. Alaska is known for high quality wild salmon and halibut. Arron enjoyed these premium products throughout his childhood. When he went to college in another state, he discovered how poor the quality of some species of fish were in the US outside of Alaska. Arron visited an expensive seafood restaurant in New York with his father and sister. They were outraged by the low quality of the so-called 'wild Alaskan salmon'. It was one big deception in their eyes. Many Americans do not like to eat fish. Arron and his family thought it might be due to the low quality of fish for sale.

Almost all (91%) seafood consumed in the United States is imported from other countries. Two-thirds of all Alaskan sustainably sourced seafood is sold to China and Japan.[51] This means that the US exports seafood of the highest quality and imports seafood of lower quality. This inspired Arron to create the 'Wild Alaskan Company', a seafood e-commerce company.

The company's mission is to make high quality and sustainably caught seafood available to American consumers who do not live in Alaska. Besides sustainability and high quality, Arron also wants to build an extremely customer-centric business. His goal is to be the prime source of seafood for his customers for life. The company is dedicated to building loyalty through fantastic quality and service.

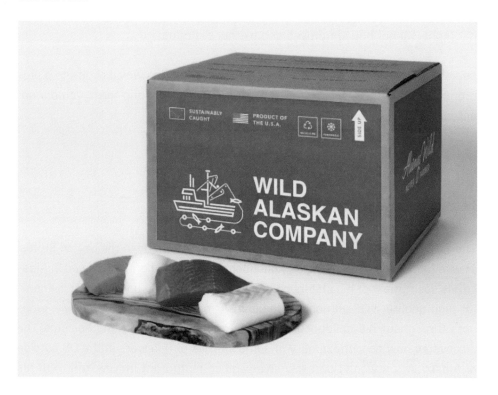

Customers can choose from a range of subscriptions that deliver fresh fish to their doorstep at regular intervals. There is a choice of wild salmon, halibut, cod and other marine species such as crab and prawns. The quality of Wild Alaskan Company's packaging and logistics is top tier. All fish is frozen immediately after being caught. It is shipped as individual vacuum-packed pieces in a box of dry ice surrounded with special packaging to ensure that the seafood is kept cool and fresh. Recipes are sent to customers every week to inspire them to enjoy this top product even more.

The company's subscription formula is completely flexible. Customers decide how many pieces of fish they want to receive each month. The scheduled delivery date for their choice is found on the company's website. This delivery time can be moved at any time to ensure that the customer is at home when their fresh fish is delivered. Subscriptions are 100% flexible. Customers can suspend their subscription if they are travelling, and no payment will be due for that month. Subscriptions can be cancelled at any time without any justification or discussion.

Customers are in for a surprise when they subscribe: 'The Captain's Cut'. This is not mentioned on the Wild Alaskan Company website. It is discovered when the customer receives their first delivery and every month members find a surprise in their order. It might be some extra pieces of salmon tail or other small pieces of fish the company does not want to sell separately. Sometimes customers find pieces of white fish ideal for making tacos. The company could make fish salad out of these offcuts or sell the pieces at a lower price but instead they give them to their customers as a little gift. Customers who order 12 pieces of fish per month are sent 16 pieces thanks to the 'Captain's Cut' programme.

I think the company's approach is brilliant. **A classical loyalty formula would be:** *'If you are a customer with us for 12 months then you get a few extra pieces of fish.'* At Wild Alaskan Company, it is just the opposite: *'We are happy that you are a customer, so we want to welcome you right away with some extras. Hope you enjoy it.'* There is no carrot that the customer must chase. Customers are rewarded with instant appreciation. Loyalty does not require the customer to make an effort; the first step in customer loyalty comes from Wild Alaskan Company. They do not have a special loyalty programme; every customer gets excellent service from day one which makes them naturally loyal.

THE CUSTOMER LOYALTY FLYWHEEL

Let us build on the philosophy that customer loyalty starts with the company, not the customer. If companies have the right philosophy and communication and take the right actions, then a customer loyalty flywheel effect develops. The expected results are clear: achieve greater customer loyalty and ensure that your customers also become your ambassadors. This is a double win: loyalty helps companies to retain its customers and the existing customers themselves become the main acquisition channel for new customers.

In the following I define the steps needed to achieve this double win. This model is not based on scientific research on customer loyalty but, instead, on my experience in the market in combination with years of consumer research.

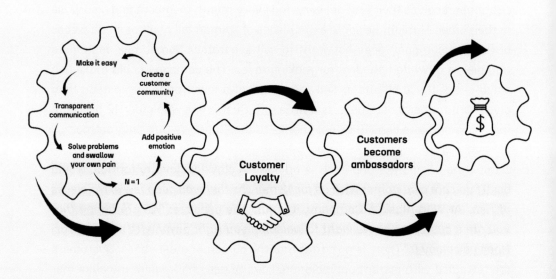

STEP 1: CONVENIENCE – MAKE LIFE EASY FOR CUSTOMERS

Starbucks has a very popular mobile app. Its main feature is that customers can order and prepay. This saves customers a lot of time when picking up their favourite drink. A topic I wrote about in previous books is that time is your customers' most scarce resource. If you succeed in helping a customer save time, you will have already made an inroad into gaining the customers' loyalty. This results in an interesting paradox: the company that saves most of your time is also the company that will get most of your time. Perhaps the most successful example of this is Amazon. Amazon saves the customer so much time that it is the reference against which other companies are judged.

'Convenience is the new loyalty,' **was a saying during my presentations for years.** If you want to achieve customer loyalty, create convenience for your customers. Why are we more loyal to Uber than to a regular taxi? *Convenience!*

Build ecosystems that increase convenience for customers. Apple is one of the most successful companies ever, thanks in part to working out a smart ecosystem. Obviously, the individual Apple products (iPhone, iPad, Mac) are high quality products, but the interface between their hardware, software and other products is flawless. The combination of the Apple Watch with the iPhone, their Apple TV offering, how they have changed the music industry, and especially the user-friendly connection between all these devices, is super convenient for the user. Once you take full advantage of that ecosystem, there is almost no turning back. The loss in ease of use would be too painful. The ecosystem increases ease of use, which means loyalty is also higher than for brands with a less easy to use and convenient ecosystem.

STEP 2: MANAGE EXPECTATIONS WITH TRANSPARENT COMMUNICATION

'Hold your right hand up and repeat after me. I solemnly affirm that the evidence to be given by me shall be the truth, the whole truth, and nothing but the truth,' is an example of an oath given in a court of law. If only it were like this in customer relations. Companies sometimes perjure themselves when communicating with clients; sometimes knowingly, sometimes unknowingly and with

the best of intentions. According to a study in the *Journal of Services Marketing*, higher customer loyalty occurs when service is accompanied by clear and transparent communication.[52] But so many companies set themselves up to fail.

Suppose a customer calls a website designer to inquire about building a new website. The customer finds the conversation useful and asks for a free, no obligation quotation. The customer is not in a hurry but wants to know how long it might take to receive the quote. This is the point where the designer can prepare for their own success or failure. Wanting to make a good impression on the customer the designer says, *'I will have that quotation ready within three days. Is that ok with you?'* To which the customer replies, *'Super!'*

The designer knows that because of supplier issues, they will not meet the promised delivery date. They finish the offer late on the 4th day after meeting the customer and send it off. So even before they have landed the job they have already – unnecessarily – disappointed the customer. **The designer could have, instead, organised their own success.**

The customer is not in a hurry but wants to know how long it might take to receive the quote. The designer replies, *'Is it ok if I send the proposal to you by the end of next week? Is that still in time for you?'* In 75% of cases, this will be fine for the customer, but you already know that you will be able to forward the quote earlier. You bought yourself some time, with the specific aim of ensuring a positive surprise. Like in the other example, four days later you send off the quote. The customer is super enthusiastic about your reliability and the fact that you are even slightly faster than what you promised.

Of course, your promise must be within reasonable market expectations. If you say, 'I can have that quote with you in four weeks', you might as well not start working on it at all. Keep a balance between promises and what is doable.

STEP 3: SOLVE PROBLEMS AND SWALLOW YOUR OWN PAIN

Are you willing to hurt yourself in the short term to gain trust in the long term? (This topic is covered in greater detail in Chapter 4.) There are moments in a customer relationship when you show your loyalty by doing something for free, or by solving a problem even if it costs you something. Think back to the philosophy of the Ritz-Carlton hotel. The value of each customer over the lifetime of the customer relationship leaves enough of a margin to make compensation of customers affordable. The Ritz-Carlton company budgets for it. Every employee is aware of the available budget and can use it at the appropriate time. Ritz-Carlton uses this philosophy because they know how much a loyal customer is worth to them. Management realises that saving 100 euro in resolving a conflict can cost thousands in the long run. The interesting thing about the Ritz-Carlton system is that compensation payments are budgeted for and included in its forecasted overheads. Because each customer does not receive a compensation payment there is always a positive effect on the bottom line. This feels good. Other companies reflect compensation payments as an unexpected loss and that does not feel good. Rather than giving worthless trinkets to customers, you may want to set up a compensation and surprise budget at your company.

STEP 4: SEGMENT SIZE = 1

Every customer is different. Every person is different. Everyone has their own needs and expectations that are more or less important. In other words, it is valuable to think of each individual customer as an individual segment.

Many data-driven companies incorporate the 'segment of 1' philosophy into their strategic planning. Players like Netflix, Spotify, Amazon and Meta want to give us the most personalised range of content and products possible. There are billions of Facebook users, but each user has an individual timeline. No two in the world are identical. The 'segment of 1' philosophy is starting to appear in more and more sectors. Think, for instance, of all the virtual personal trainer apps. Based on your profile, you get a personalised workout schedule. Sephora, a cosmetics and beauty products retailer, offers personalised beauty advice to its customers. This philosophy is also increasingly becoming a tried-and-tested concept in B2B markets. Atlas Copco, a global compressor manufacturer, can learn much more about how end users interact with their products thanks to data. 'Segment of 1' data will enable them to offer proactive and personalised service that can significantly increase user satisfaction and loyalty.

STEP 5: NURTURE POSITIVE EMOTION

You can do your job well but still fail to create a positive emotion in the customer. Lasting positive emotions are needed to activate the customer loyalty flywheel. A favourite book on the topic of customer experience is Dan and Chip Heath's book, *The Power of Moments*. They explain that every step in a customer relationship does not have to be an unforgettable and perfect moment. They use the example of a visit to Disney World.

If you were to dissect the entire day of a visit to Disney World and determine a satisfaction score for various parts of the day, the overall satisfaction score might be low. Imagine a typical day in Disney World. You get up and rush to the park very early to be at the gates to the Magic Kingdom when they open. But when you arrive, you find hundreds of people at the entrance. It seems some people have woken up even earlier than you have!

You finally enter and stroll down Main Street USA. There is a pleasant feeling in the air. You decide to take in some attractions and brave yet more long queues to enjoy rides that last only a few minutes. But then it is time for Splash Mountain, a highlight of the day. You and your family have worked up an appetite. You buy an expensive lunch of irritatingly average quality food. After lunch you hit the queues again to experience more attractions. Finally comes the undisputed highlight of a day at Disney: an impressive fireworks display accompanied by beautiful soundtracks from many Disney classic films. If you were to grade your visit from 1-10 for each attraction or experience in terms of satisfaction, the average score might be 6.5/10. However, the reality is that Disney World's satisfaction scores are a lot higher. Most people rate their visits to Disney World as fantastic, awarding scores of 9/10 or higher. Why is this? The answer is that overall satisfaction reflects *'the power of moments'*. **You do not need to have a top score for every interaction to elicit an overall positive emotion. A good 'highlight' and a good transition (end of interaction) are important.** Your emotional response to Splash Mountain (highlight) and the fireworks at the end of the day (highlight and transition) provided that positive emotion.

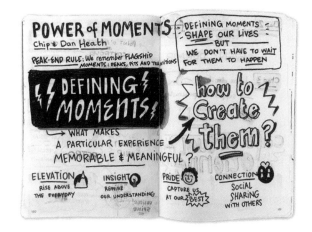

In other words, to create positive emotion, customers do not have to score your company excellent on everything, but you must choose your moments well. If someone wants to buy a car, make sure the moment of requesting the offer and picking up the new car are top moments. Do everything you can to make those moments unforgettable. If you work in construction: make sure the first site meeting and the delivery are great. Do not let these be simply transactional moments, find creative ways to make them highlights. You can check to ensure that your customers respond with a positive emotion.

STEP 6: BUILD A COMMUNITY OF ENTHUSIASTIC CUSTOMERS

Companies that manage to build a community of enthusiastic customers have the strongest possible customer loyalty. Supporters of football teams (who are in fact customers) have extremely high levels of loyalty to their team (the company/brand). Supporters even speak about their team in the 'we' form. 'We' are playing Champions League against Benfica this week. 'We' have recruited a new player. Certain fantasy figures or worlds also have very large fan communities. Think, for example, of Star Wars or Harry Potter fans. Years after the last Harry Potter book and film was released, anything linked to the young wizard is still a huge success. Both online and physically, these fans are up in arms almost daily to defend their favourite heroes. When a new product or event associated with their team or hero arrives, these fans are the biggest ambassadors to support its promotion.

When brands manage to build a community amongst their customers, there is a positive effect on loyalty. According to McKinsey, there is also a direct effect on financial results. Brands with a strong community can charge higher prices, have less need for promotions and have lower advertising costs.[53]

Lululemon, a retailer with a focus on sportswear, has chosen the creation of a supporter base as a deliberate marketing strategy. Lululemon's mission is to ensure that everyone can feel and look good. To succeed in that mission, they sell fun, sporty clothing. They also bought technology company, Mirror, in 2020. Mirror sells smart mirrors that serve as personal trainers. While people are working out, they can monitor data that describes their performance in the mirror. The Mirror provides enough data to make it seem like the Mirror is your personal trainer, that helps with your training from the comfort of your own home without other people around. Many analysts thought Lululemon's purchase of Mirror was an odd acquisition, asking why would a retail company buy a technology company now? If you think back to Lululemon's mission – everyone should feel good and be able to look good – this acquisition is a logical move. You can make people look good through your fashion products but also through regular workouts.

In 2022, Lululemon launched their own community. The purchase of a Mirror subscription for USD 39 monthly entitled the customer to free community membership or one could buy community membership-only for USD 39 per month. The benefits for free members were faster access to new products and invitations to live community events. There was also a paid formula where members pay USD 39 per month. That was the same price as a subscription to Mirror. In other words, existing Mirror customers immediately became members of the paying community. To convince other customers, they offered a lot of free clothes so that the membership fee was almost earned back with these free clothes. Besides the discounts and financial benefits, the aim was to build a real lifestyle community. Members could meet regularly for fitness classes or yoga sessions in the shops. The Lululemon programme went beyond a classic loyalty programme. It brought people together with similar interests. In time, they want to make the community even stronger, and it will become the central part of their customer loyalty strategy. In mid-2023, Lululemon took the decision to part ways with Mirror again. Interest in the Mirror hardware was not as high as expected, with customers proving particularly interested in the physical meetings and exercising in a social context. Despite a parting of ways with Mirror, the community continues.

Companies are setting up communities even in B2B markets. Human8 (formerly InSites Consulting) is one of the leading companies in the market research industry (B2B services). They have more than 1.000 employees and their offices are spread across every continent. I know the company very well having worked there myself for 12 years, for most of that time as one of the organisation's managing partners. In my view, Human8 has always been an example of a B2B company that was able to engage customers in a very clever way. Its marketing philosophy is very powerful: it is not about us, it's about our customers. Human8's customers are featured in most of their marketing communications. This can be in the form of blog articles, podcasts, videos or presentations at industry events. Each time, a customer is profiled in a positive way. The most powerful form of Human8's community building is the collaboration between customers and their R&D department. Customers have the chance to participate in projects where new, innovative, market research techniques are developed. This way, the customer has participated in an financially beneficial research project, and they learn about the latest developments in the field from a front row seat. If the project is a success, the result may be a joint presentation at an industry event. The ultimate effect is that customers learn from customers. Working with a company that develops new knowledge independently of commercial projects is very valuable. Working with a company that connects clients facing the same challenges enriches your career. Thus, working with them more becomes valuable and loyalty increases.

A company can supply its customers with content and activities, and it can also act as a facilitator. I am a co-founder of Nexxworks. Our company's mission is to encourage our clients to invest a structural part of their resources (time and money) in 'the day after tomorrow'. One of our most successful products is inspiration trips. Over the past decade, we have taken hundreds of business leaders on trips to the most innovative hubs of our planet (San Francisco, Los Angeles, Berlin, Oslo, Tokyo, Dubai, Singapore, Beijing, Shanghai...) to seek inspiration from the most innovative companies and people of our generation from the front row. Over the past few years, we have endeavoured to transform this group of people into a community. Many of our inspiration travellers meet regularly at community events where we share new inspirations. Clients have met one another through Nexxworks and seek inspiration from one another. In short, we facilitate a community of company leaders who believe in innovation and extreme customer focus. We will continue to meet one another on this path to the future.

FROM LOYALTY PROGRAMME TO A COMMUNITY

Online communities increasingly determine whether something will become a success. For example, if a book is picked up by #booktok on TikTok, the chances of it becoming a bestseller increase. In addition, the higher a book scores in this community the higher its chances of being adapted into a film. Building an enthusiastic book community is an opportunity that is being overlooked by almost every publisher and bookstore. Most regions have an important online book platform and the reviews and conversations on such platforms determine the success of a book. Consider the opportunity this presents for traditional book shops for example. In most cases, these retailers still use a classic loyalty card system: if you buy a lot of books, you are entitled to a discount from us (much) later. If the bookstores were instead focused on building a community, the community could act as flywheel for building customer loyalty. Instead of always rethinking classic loyalty programmes, it makes much more sense to think about building a customer community.

BUILDING A CUSTOMER COMMUNITY

The community is the last and most crucial part of the customer loyalty flywheel. So, in the following I will describe the various strategies one can use to build a customer community.

COMMUNITY STRATEGY 1: MEMBERSHIPS

I personally think Lululemon's membership is a better example of building a community than Amazon Prime. Why do I think this? Of course, Amazon Prime is very successful, but it is mainly driven by the economic and rational benefits associated with membership. Customers get discounts, faster deliveries, a subscription to Prime Video and other benefits. However, the memberships are 'independent', meaning members are not in contact with one another. So, membership in Amazon Prime does not actively build an Amazon community. Contrast this with Lululemon's strategy where membership provides access to exclusive membership events where members can meet one another. Members usually have similar interests, and this creates a bond between customers. This is the way to build a community. Members could also be given a voice in company decisions. If customers' inputs and feedback are visibly considered, the bonds with the company are reinforced.

It is crucial that members meet either physically or online to use membership as the foundation of a customer community. When the bond between members is facilitated by the company this can enhance loyalty to the company.

COMMUNITY STRATEGY 2: WEB3 TECHNOLOGY

Web3 is a new phase of the internet. Web1 involved posting and transmitting information via the internet. Web2 was the phase where users themselves could actively share content and have a real voice. In this phase, companies like Facebook, Tripadvisor and YouTube emerged. Content was no longer posted by a few; everyone could share content themselves. Web2 sent a shockwave through the world of customer experience. The voice of the consumer suddenly resounded as if through a megaphone, increasing the pressure for a better customer experience. My first book *The Conversation Manager* was about this digital evolution.

Web1 and Web2 were based on a centralised model with a few organisations having most of the power. For example, our data is owned by a few large companies over which we, as consumers, have little control. If we want to buy or sell things, we are dependent on those central platforms. Web3 is a decentralised internet that will use Blockchain technology, enabling users to manage their own data and transactions without the intervention of a third party. I will not go into the more technical and complex aspects of Web3, but rather the impact that Web3 can have on customer relationships and customer loyalty.

A concrete example is the potential of NFTs to boost customer loyalty. An NFT (non-fungible token) is a unique digital asset created on a blockchain, such as Ethereum. Unlike traditional cryptocurrencies, like Bitcoin or Ethereum, NFTs are not interchangeable as they each have unique characteristics and features that distinguish them from other NFTs. This makes them ideal for representing digital objects that are unique, such as artworks, music, videos, memes and other digital content. Perhaps the best-known example of NFTs are the Bored Apes, which are drawings of cartoon images sold for a lot of money as NFTs. If someone buys such an NFT, that person is the sole owner of that unique image, meaning that the buyer owns not only the artwork but also the smart contract and intellectual rights linked to that NFT. Some Bored Ape NFT holders have started making money from derivatives of their NFT via the sale of T-shirts for example, others have even co-opted a Bored Ape hamburger chain and yet another group has agreed sponsorship deals with big companies like Adidas. Smart contracts like these are key to increasing customer loyalty.

Imagine you are a talented singer songwriter, but you cannot find a record company that will work with you. In the old world, it would have been game over. In the world of NFTs, there is an alternative. Most young talent already have a large group of followers on social media (TikTok, Instagram, YouTube). As a result, you can release your first music as an NFT. In the smart contract, you can include as an added benefit that, for example, 10% of your royalties will be divided among the NFT holders. This is a brilliant deal for artists. Record companies normally take about 90% of the proceeds from their artists under contract. Artists do most of the promo themselves, these days. This makes the traditional model unsustainable. **In contrast, the NFT model is a good deal for the artist, but also for the first fans. The more successful the artist becomes, the more money the first fans make thanks to their NFTs. Imagine if you had bought Ed Sheeran's first music that way and you were entitled to a percentage of his royalties! Then you might not be reading this book right now.** Fans are almost like shareholders. Chances are these people will become more than fans and might well become your biggest ambassadors, considering they benefit financially themselves.

This NFT strategy does not work everywhere. Three conditions are needed for it to succeed:
1. Scarcity: the number of NFT's must be limited to protect their value.
2. Smart contract: a smart contract must be linked to the purchase of an NFT. This contract provides additional value to the buyer beyond just ownership of the creative asset.
3. Community: a pre-existing community of fans is needed to create enthusiasm around an NFT collection. People should be proud to buy one of your NFTs, so to speak.

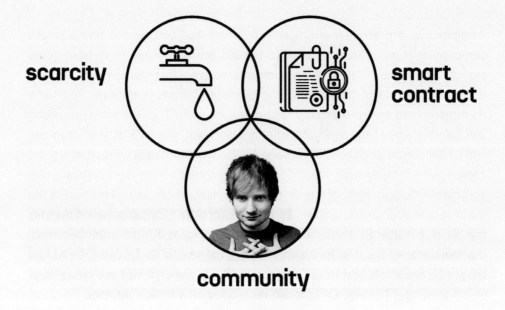

scarcity

smart contract

community

The idea of co-ownership boosts connection with brands, increasing loyalty. NFT holders also often have the chance to meet at physical events or may speak to one another via Discord (a social network) which also builds a community among this group of ambassadors.

COMMUNITY STRATEGY 3:
ACTIVATE YOUR AMBASSADORS

Recognising active customers can create a community of loyal fans. Many brands provide their fans with visual support to show their fan-ship. Apple has several wallpapers that fans can use on their phones or their Macs. The fact that Apple packages a sticker with iPhones supplies customers with an emblem to show that they belong to the Apple community. Starbucks has several templates for use on Instagram and Snapchat filters that fans can use to share their love for Starbucks online. Visible symbols of fan-ship help fans to easily find one another. They are often conversation starters with other brand fans.

Some brands go a step further and activate their fans to become part of an active brand community. These communities can, for instance, undertake a part of customer service, or inspire other customers about which products would suit them. For example, Lululemon has a community of brand ambassadors called 'The Sweat Collective', in addition to their membership formula (described previously). The Sweat Collective helps organise events and campaigns. Cosmetics retailer Sephora has the 'Sephora Squad'. These people help run campaigns and create content for the company. They are rewarded with exclusive access to new products, events and even certain training courses. The line between these customers and an engaged employee can become very narrow. Working together helps to build an active community of very loyal customers.

COMMUNITY STRATEGY 4: FACILITATE CONTENT SHARING

You can invite people to share certain brand-related content by making it easy, fun or valuable for them. The easiest way to motivate people is to give them something. Shopee is a popular e-commerce platform in Southeast Asia that regularly runs competitions and promotions where customers are encouraged to post photos of themselves with a Shopee purchase. Some of them get extra rewards for doing so. Most people do this for the personal benefit, which means the content gets shared, but there is no real community to drive customer loyalty.

Shein goes a step further. Shein, a Chinese company, is currently one of the most successful fashion platforms in the world. In 2022, Shein's sales were around USD 30 billion.[54] By comparison, H&M had sales of just over USD 20 billion that year and Zara had sales of about USD 35 billion. In the United States, there are currently more smartphones with the Shein app installed on them than phones with the Amazon app.[55] But there is controversy surrounding Shein, such as concerns about the ethical correctness of the company (their prices are so low that it brings into question how this is done) and about their negative impact on the climate (their cheap goods encourage a disposable society). A study of Shein's marketing strategy shows the importance of content sharing by their loyal customers. Every customer is encouraged to write reviews about the products they buy. Reviewers receive five Shein points for each review and 100 points equals a USD 1 discount. Thousands of young girls are preoccupied by writing reviews that can earn them free clothing.

At both Shopee and Shein, customers share a lot of content, but neither leads to the creation of a real customer community. Communities of customers need to believe in your mission and your message. Once customers start sharing things from the heart and talking to each other, only then can a community develop; only then can a community of customers stimulate lasting customer loyalty. In a recent blog, Ken Hughes, my fellow customer experience speaker and writer, described a brilliant example: Taylor Swift.[56] When she launched her 'Anti-Hero' single in early 2023, she motivated her fans to share content with one another. **When a new song comes out, an artist always posts the video on YouTube, fans watch it a few times and that's it. Taylor Swift went beyond this classic approach.** Through YouTube Shorts (videos of one minute maximum), she launched the #TSAntiHeroChallenge. Anti-Hero is a song about what you do not like about yourself. Swift invited fans to make short videos, describing what they do not like about themselves. Fans do this in a sincere or joking fashion. Taylor led by example by posting a video on the Anti-Hero Challenge herself. This motivated fans to share their own Anti-Hero feelings and stories, daring to show themselves as they are.

THE CUSTOMER FLYWHEEL IN ACTION: B&M OPTICS!

The customer loyalty flywheel has two main effects. The faster the wheel spins, the greater customer loyalty becomes and the more your customers become active ambassadors of your company.

One of the best examples of a customer loyalty flywheel in action is Belgium's B&M optics. This shop – one of the most successful opticians in Belgium and an example of a polished diamond – is operated by Ingrid Brackx and her husband Luc Mangodt. Ingrid and Luc have customer-oriented business in their genes. A few years ago, they completely rethought their business. Since then, B&M optics' slogan has been 'Optics by Day, Wine and Art by Night'. Their shop is still a beautiful optics shop but is also an art gallery where local artists can exhibit their works and it is also a wine bar where wine lovers can enjoy a fine selection of quality wines.

Optics by day, wine and art by night

STEP 1: MAKE LIFE EASY FOR YOUR CUSTOMERS

B&M optics' door is always open, and everyone is welcome. Customers who are waiting for a service (repairing glasses, sizing a lens) are not asked to come back later. Instead, they are invited to wait in the shop over a cup of coffee, a soft drink, or a glass of wine. Free WIFI and a customer toilet are available in the shop. Within 30 minutes, their repair is done. Sometimes people wander in out of curiosity and fall in love with a new pair of frames. If they buy a new frame on the spur of the moment, the B&M team puts their lenses into the new frame within half an hour. An eye test takes 10 minutes; tailoring lenses to fit a new spectacle frame takes 15 minutes. B&M customers save time, compared to other opticians, and enjoy relaxing in the shop during the short wait for their new glasses.

Ingrid and Luc make every effort to make life easier for their customers. Their credo is: 'Once you buy glasses from us, you don't have to worry about them anymore.' If they find that a customer needs a visit to the ophthalmologist, they make the appointment for them and all the documents they need for that visit are filled out for them and sent to their home. An eyewear cleaning product and lens tissues are free of charge and refilled free of charge. When customers come back to the shop for refills, Ingrid and Luc can check their glasses. As a result, problems are solved even before the customer notices there is a problem.

STEP 2: MANAGE EXPECTATIONS WITH TRANSPARENT COMMUNICATION

If a customer chooses a particular frame and the B&M team thinks the model does not fit the customer very well, it can lead to an awkward conversation. The easiest thing to do would be to say nothing or to agree with the customer that the frames suit them, but that would not lead to customer loyalty in the long run. Instead, the B&M team explains as diplomatically as possible to the customer why they believe the frames do not suit them. Something like, 'Imagine you see someone on television wearing glasses that are too pronounced, you might miss much of what that person says because you are distracted by their glasses.' Often that is enough for customers to consider another model.

STEP 3: SOLVE PROBLEMS AND ABSORB THE COSTS

Customer who have a problem with their glasses may arrive in a somewhat disgruntled mood. Many people have become sceptical because of the poor service they receive from the numerous rough diamond companies. So, they sometimes assume that if they have a problem, it will not be solved to their satisfaction. At B&M, 'No problem, let me take care of that for you,' is invariably the opening line.

For instance, children's glasses must be changed every two years on average. B&M offers a full three-year guarantee on frames and lenses with the purchase of every new pair of children's glasses, ensuring that that the risk of damage lies entirely with B&M and not with the customer. If a frame is damaged beyond repair, they will propose to grind the lenses to fit into a new frame so that the customer is not left without glasses. 'Children are our future,' is the underlying message.

If a defect is discovered during a service, B&M will immediately order a replacement part as needed. The repair happens even before the customer notices they have a problem and again, repairs to glasses purchased at B&M are done under guarantee. When the customer is informed that they need not pay for the repair, only then do some admit that they dropped their glasses, but dared not bring it up because the damage was their own fault.

B&M's service is very reliable and their way of communicating with customers is very smart. Their philosophy is to never argue with customers. They replace defective parts for free anyway, so there is no point in proving themselves right before making the repair. Their overall goal is that customers leave the shop satisfied and with a positive impression. **Luc has observed** *'Companies spend so much money on advertising, but the cost of helping a customer is much less than the cost of an ad and delivers much more.'*

STEP 4: SEGMENT SIZE = 1

A personalised sales approach can make every customer feel good, but B&M has found a way to improve on this, to add an extra personal touch. Prescriptions are engraved on lenses, visible only if the glasses are held at a certain angle. B&M asks their lens suppliers to engrave the customer's initials on the lens as well. The engraving is shown to the customers when they collect their glasses. This touch of personalisation is something that customers enjoy, demonstrating that the glasses were made especially for them and not mass-produced as they are by large optical chains.

STEP 5: CREATE POSITIVE EMOTION

B&M offers a unique experience thanks to the addition of art and a wine bar to their core optical business. They optimise the overall customer experience by working with wine and art experts. A specialised wine shop runs the wine bar, organises tasting evenings and collaborates on events. Local artists provide beautiful sculptures and other decorative objects and Professor Willem Elias, a local art expert, acts as curator, assembling beautiful art collections. B&M's concept of 'Optics by Day; Wine and Art by Night,' has transformed the shop into a destination. Normally a customer goes to an optical shop only when it is necessary. People visit B&M for the events and the experience. I remember visiting the shop on one of the stormiest Saturdays of the year. I did not expect to find many people there, given the terrible weather. A jazz band was playing as I entered, the wine bar was full of people and others were admiring the artwork. The vibes were wonderful, and everyone felt the positive emotion. The whole concept and atmosphere made it more than a visit to a shop, and I travelled home with positive feelings.

STEP 6: BUILD A COMMUNITY OF ENTHUSIASTIC CUSTOMERS

An optical shop can also build a community. At B&M, events are the main tool for this. They regularly organise wine tastings and vernissages in their shop. No proactive commercial effort is made on those evenings, because the aim is only to give people a good time. Of course, guests may also discover the B&M's optical products, and this often leads to a pair of glasses being sold in parallel with a wine tasting. It happens almost automatically. Many people return with friends; a route for expanding the community. 'My next pair of glasses will definitely come from here,' is a comment that Ingrid and Luc hear quite often during evenings in the shop.

POLISHED DIAMONDS GIVE
BUT EXPECT NOTHING IN RETURN

As you can probably sense, I am very excited by the story of B&M. To my mind, B&M shows that any company can succeed in becoming a polished diamond. If the mindset, communication and actions are right, it is achievable for everyone.

Sincere customer loyalty is a fundamental prerequisite for being a polished diamond. Rough diamond companies too often harbour a traditional view of customer loyalty (How can we make the customer more loyal to our company?). Rough diamonds too often engage in awkward discussions with customers or make things unnecessarily difficult for the customer. Polished diamonds know that customer loyalty results from investing in the various elements of the customer loyalty flywheel. Polished diamond companies believe that respecting the value of and nurturing good customer relations will eventually be reflected in its financial returns.

WILL I STILL MAKE A PROFIT IF I
PAMPER THE CUSTOMER LIKE THIS?

There are still many managers who assign a cost to customer focus, thinking that it only has a cost but no financial return. I always find this a strange perspective. Consider the following financial benefits of high customer loyalty and very happy customers:

- ◆ Attracting new customers is more expensive than retaining existing ones. Thus, high customer loyalty means less pressure on sales and results because you already start with a solid financial buffer.
- ◆ Loyal customers elevate your reputation, increase word-of-mouth promotion and all this makes it easier to attract new customers.
- ◆ Customer focus reduces customer service costs because the better your service, the fewer problems there are to solve.

However, it is very important to look very closely at one aspect of the marketing mix to protect your company's profits. Price! One of the best customer experience books of recent years is *The Customer Leader*, written by Rudy Moenaert and Henry Robben. The book includes a brilliant piece about managing price in your customer relationship.

Customer-centricity does not equal cheap prices; quite the contrary. Usually, the products of customer-centric companies are more expensive. Customers of companies that excel in customer-centricity are willing to pay more. A Salesforce study showed that 66% of customers are willing to pay more for a good experience.[57] A study by American Express shows that consumers are willing to pay up to 17% more for product or service from a company with excellent customer focus.[58] In other words, as a polished diamond (in the making), you need not be afraid to set your price high. *The Customer Leader* is the title of a McK-

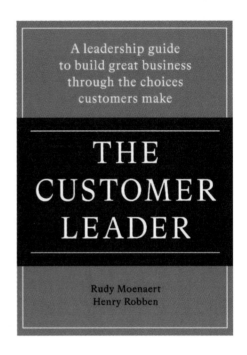

A leadership guide to build great business through the choices customers make

THE CUSTOMER LEADER

Rudy Moenaert
Henry Robben

insey study that measured the impact of price on profitability. The study (on some 1.000 medium-sized US companies) showed that fixed costs account for about 19% of sales, variable costs up to 64% and operating profit averages 17%. The McKinsey researchers then built a price simulation model which resulted in impressive insights.[59]

- ◆ If revenue increases by 1%, operating profit increases by 2.1%.
- ◆ Reducing fixed costs by 1% increases operating profit by 1.1%.
- ◆ Reducing variable costs by 1% increases operating profit by 3.8%.
- ◆ Increasing prices by 1% leads to a 6% increase in operating profit!

Raising prices leads to higher profit than reducing variable and fixed costs, combined!

As a polished diamond with very loyal customers, it would be a shame to set your price too low. Of course, you should not price yourself out of the market, but unnecessary discounts or positioning yourself too cheap leads to a needless loss.

Rudy Moenaert and Henry Robben describe three mistaken justifications for lowering prices:

i. The spectre of competition. The reality is that just about every sector experiences pressure on prices. Competition is keen everywhere. What happens if a pure price player enters your market? The pressure on price increases even more. Successful companies convince the customer to purchase based on value, not price. If a cheap price is your only selling point, you usually do not have enough value to offer in other aspects of your product. After a (very expensive) visit to Disneyland, the customer will have forgotten the price they paid but they will remember the value they received for months afterwards. Don't be blinded by aggressive competitor pricing, offer enough value and keep your customer experience high to make up the difference in prices.

ii. Commissions. Many industries attempt to motivate their salespeople by paying them in part or entirely by commission on sales. **If you reward sales success, you will get it but at a cost.** Commission based remuneration motivates salespeople to reduce the price to increase the potential to make a sale. Their attempts to meet their sales targets translates into lowered profitability.

iii. The spectre of alternative suppliers. Many companies fear that customers will switch to an alternative supplier. A lower price may keep a customer on board for a while, but ultimately most customers will choose the supplier offering the best value and the best customer experience. Focus on value creation and not low price.

Our brains and our egos can complicate discussions about prices. Suppose your company offers professional services and 50% of your offers convert into contracts. That is quite a good conversion rate. But inevitably the question of price will come up. Why is that? Because it is an easy target. The debate goes like this: if you win a lot of contracts then your price is too low and if you lose too many offers, then your price is too high. It is far more difficult yet far more important to get to the root of the reason why you are successful and do more of it or determine why you are not more successful and either correct the problem or stop repeating it.

This chapter is about customer loyalty. Data proves that loyal and satisfied customers are willing to pay more. Is that going to convince everyone? Not at all. 'If you try to please everyone, you'll please no one,' actor Ricky Gervais once said. Radiant diamonds do not want to excite everyone in the world, but rather the customers who fit their proposition. By charging the right price, you will ensure that your efforts in customer loyalty also result in higher profitability. A company's mission is to create value for customers and the corollary is to create value for shareholders. This way, you will achieve both objectives.

*People don't like to say they found the salesman annoying or read **bad feedback** on the internet.*

CONCRETE CUSTOMER EXPERIENCE TIPS FROM THIS CHAPTER:

1. Find a way to bring customers together around a common interest that reflects the core of your business.
2. Activate customers to act as ambassadors of your company: motivate them by involving them in decisions and give them information to share about the company.
3. Involve your customers in content creation and sharing. Make it as easy and valuable as possible for customers to share content about your company.
4. Think of a way to stimulate positive emotions in your customer relationships.
5. Do not be afraid to share expertise for free. Do so without any short-term expectations.
6. Do not promise your clients the impossible; be realistic. Better to promise you will send a quote within 1.5 weeks (which is perfectly acceptable for most customers) but send it to them after 5 days, than to promise it within 3 days, when they end up having to wait 5 days.
7. Do not expect your customers to be loyal to you. Loyalty begins with the company, with you. Be loyal to your customers.
8. View customer focus as an ongoing, long-term philosophy. Sometimes you will have to hurt yourself a little in the short term to benefit yourself – along with your customer, of course – later.

CHAPTER 6

EFFECTIVE EMPATHY

'DON'T DO BIG THINGS. DO LOTS OF SMALL THINGS, **WITH GREAT LOVE**'

MOTHER TERESA

A BAD SYSTEM WILL BEAT
A GOOD PERSON EVERY TIME

It promised to be a beautiful Saturday evening. We were on our way to a good restaurant to enjoy a pleasant evening with friends. On the way to our rendez-vous, we suddenly drove through a pothole that was a lot deeper and harder than we expected. The jolt set off the car alarm and 'Stop the car immediately' began to flash on the dashboard. Since we were only two kilometres from the restaurant, we decided to drive on anyway. When we arrived, we found that one of our tyres was punctured. It would be impossible to drive the car home after dinner. This was a new situation for me. I had never used road assistance before, but there was no alternative.

My body was already starting to tremble a little as I dialled the call centre. I saw our beautiful evening passing me by as I hung on the line for half an hour, waiting for the voice of salvation. To my delight, the response was rapid. Our details were noted, and we were promised assistance within the hour. Mean-while, we sat down at the table with a story to start the conversation. About 45 minutes later, a waiter alerted me that someone from VAB road assistance had arrived. When I went outside, I met a super friendly man who had already seen the problem. *'If you will give me your keys, sir, we will sort this out for you as efficiently as possible so that you can enjoy your meal. I will take your car for repair and return with a replacement car in 30 minutes. Your car will be taken to your regular garage by Monday at the latest.'* Well-organised and friendly service and a replacement car. Impressive.

A car, of the same make as our car, arrived as promised. It was even an au-tomatic, like ours. The VAB-man said, **'Everything will be fine, sir, have a nice evening,'** as he left on a new mission to help someone else with car trouble. I was extremely impressed at how smoothly it all went and at the courtesy of the VAB employee. We discussed this positive experience with our friends over din-ner. One of the people at the table was Rudy Moenaert (referred to in Chapter 5). Rudy is a highly regarded professor of strategic marketing at TiasNimbas Busi-ness School, Tilburg University, The Netherlands. I am repeatedly impressed by his sharp analyses and extensive knowledge of the marketing literature.

Immediately Rudy quoted W. Edwards Deming[60] who had observed that, *'A bad system will beat a good person every time!'* Then Rudy remarked, *'That VAB fellow can do as good a job as he wants, but if his company's systems are not well organised, he will bump up against limits in his ability to provide good service.'* Since that evening, I have been a big fan of VAB and of the Deming quote that Rudy introduced me to.

You can employ the most competent people, but if they are hampered in delivering excellent service by the lack of well-oiled processes and systems, those people will become frustrated. Customers will not be satisfied, and good employees will leave the company. This creates negative spirals. VAB's processes are excellent, and their people are motivated and together this creates a positive spiral.

Rough diamonds do not always have the most streamlined processes and customer interactions. Polished diamonds have processes that work well and have the mental flexibility to not always stick to them 100%. Remember one of the first examples in this book, the story of the marriage proposal at Disneyland Paris that went wrong? Disney has excellent processes, but in that case they stuck too rigidly to the process. Guests are not allowed on that stage, so whatever the situation may be, they are removed from it very quickly. That is a logical and well-thought-out rule. Only you need the empathy to realise that a marriage proposal might be a justifiable exception. Radiant diamond companies train their employees to execute processes flawlessly AND invite them to dare to make a decision that colours outside the lines of the process at the right time.

PANIC ON 31-12-21

Business processes are in continuous evolution. It is a never-ending story about acting with speed, empathy and decisiveness. I was in Dubai to visit the World Expo in 2021. My family was travelling with me. The expo was very inspiring, and the trip was extra exciting because it was my first major overseas expedition after the COVID lockdowns. It was a fantastic experience!

We had scheduled our return flight on 1 January 2022. We had a fun New Year's Eve planned with other frequent travellers before heading to the airport. You may remember that COVID infection was still a risk in that timeframe. We had to be meticulous about having all the right documents to travel, vaccinations... The good news first: everyone in our party was vaccinated which meant we did not need proof of a recent negative COVID test to fly back to Belgium. At the time of the trip, our youngest son was 10 years old. A vaccine had not yet been approved for his age group. Fortunately, children under 12 didn't need a negative test, so he could board the plane. We were reassured that we could travel back to Belgium worry-free.

We were in Dubai city centre when (now the bad news) we received an email from Lufthansa at 16:15 on 31 December; yes, the afternoon before our flight and it was New Year's Eve. Ever since that day, my blood pressure rises a little whenever I receive an email from Lufthansa. We were informed, in no uncertain terms, that according to the German authorities and Lufthansa the rules had changed. Our son needed a recent negative COVID test to fly the next day. I saw red. It was New Year's Eve, quarter past four in the afternoon and at seven the New Year's Eve festivities were scheduled to begin. I immediately started calling around to try to book a test. No luck. We tried a few walk-in clinics, but the queues were endless. Evi, my wife, came up with a good idea: **'Call our hotel, maybe they can help!'**

I called our hotel immediately. *'Indeed, Mr Van Belleghem, it will be very difficult to have a COVID test in the city and be back in time for the start of dinner here tonight.'* My heart sank.

'But please don't panic. We are here to help you. By what time can you make it back to the hotel?' *'6 pm,'* I said hopefully.

'May we send a doctor to your room for a COVID test at 6.15 pm?' *'Yes, of course!'* My relief could no doubt be felt at the other end of the line.

The hotel employee chuckled and said, *'Glad I could help. See you later!'*

By 6pm, we were back at the hotel. At 6.15pm there was a knock on the door. A friendly doctor came in and performed the test. Fifteen minutes later, we got the good news: a negative result.

'How would you like us to pay,' I asked, 'cash or card?' The doctor smiled and said, 'The hotel told me how stressful this situation has been for you. There will be no charge. Happy New Year!' And away she went. We were tremendously relieved and ready for the New Year's Eve celebration beginning half an hour later.

THE CUSTOMER EXPERIENCE RITUAL AT ATLANTIS, THE PALM, DUBAI

You might not find the above story so extraordinary, but I can tell you that for me, it was not the first time I unexpectedly needed a COVID test. In all other hotels and situations, I was left to my own devices by my hotel. Some hotels immediately said they could not help, others tried to arrange something ad hoc but ultimately explained that they could not help. **For me, the help from the Atlantis, The Palm hotel in Dubai was a moment of excellent customer service at a time when it really mattered to me.**

Whenever I experience excellent service, I always try to find out exactly how it is managed. I met the CEO of The Palm, Tom Roelens. We had a fantastic chat about customer-centricity. If you want to listen to my conversation with Tom, check out my podcast channel (CX Update).

The Palm hotel employs around 18.000 employees, of which 9.000 had been recruited in the six months before my visit. It is always a challenge is to acclimatise employees to the customer experience flow of a new company. This made me even more impressed with their service levels.

One of the success factors ensuring The Palm's customer experience strategy is its daily customer experience meeting. Every morning (for a hotel, that is seven days out of seven), Tom sits down with his key staff to go over the past day's customer queries. The Atlantis The Palm hotel has hundreds of customer experience processes running, but every day new, unexpected questions arise from their guests. The customer experience meeting provides a venue to review those questions. They divide them into two categories: (1) questions they do not have an existing process for, but which could apply to many customers, (2) questions they do not have a process for but are so specific that they have no value for other customers.

discuss new customer
requests and questions

normal
operations and
customer
processes

daily CX
meeting

add to the
existing process
in a structural
way

ad hoc request:
figure out how to help

My COVID query fell under the first category of queries. When a category 1 query is received, employees try to implement a new process the same day to respond to the query and solve any associated problem. The excellent service response to my COVID query was a result of this way of working. I was not the first person who needed help with arranging a COVID test. In response, the hotel had decided to assemble a group of about 30 doctors that could be available to perform COVID tests any time of day. The proactive mindset of the hotel's management makes for excellent customer service. Most other hotels will call a doctor as needed to support their customers, but in the absence of a prearranged agreement, the doctor is often not available, and the customer is left disappointed.

Even with a category two query, The Palm will try to help the customer (except if the query is illegal or unsafe). You can imagine them getting strange requests at The Palm. **They might not always able to respond successfully to a category two query, but they respond with a positive intention, and this will be appreciated by the customer.**

EFFECTIVE EMPATHY

The daily customer experience ritual at Atlantis The Palm can be described as 'effective empathy'. Every day, they hear the changing needs of the market and proactively respond to them. Empathy is probably the word most often used in customer experience or marketing presentations. **'You need to be empathetic towards your customers,'** audiences are told. I recommended this in my presentations for years, until someone in the audience asked me: *'But what form does empathy take? How does one make this intention tangible?'* I came up with an answer, but deep down I was not satisfied with it. Empathy can be defined but how can it be expressed?

I would like to use this book to launch the concept of 'effective empathy', inspired by the way of doing things at the Atlantis The Palm hotel. Effective empathy is my proposal on how to install a rapid feedback loop that results very quickly in an action. Effective empathy typifies the polished diamonds.

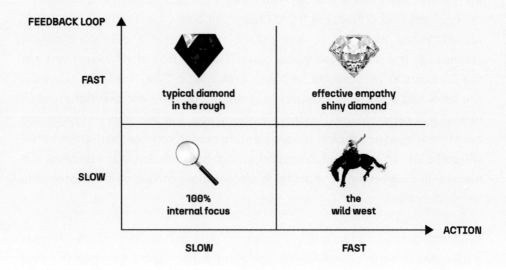

QUICK TO GATHER DATA, SLOW TO TAKE ACTION

If you are reading this book, chances are you have a higher-than-average interest in customer-centricity. Perhaps you work in a company where there is a real desire to help customers in an excellent way. Therefore, it is likely that there is already a feedback loop in your company. Many of you will conduct customer satisfaction surveys or have NPS trackers that collect the necessary data on customer experience. With rough diamonds, it often stops there. Data analyses take a long time. Before any action is taken, there is a need for a load of presentations and spreadsheets. It may take six months before the feedback loop is in place. This combination – quick gathering of feedback and slow action – typifies the rough diamonds.

TOO BUSY FOCUSING TO LISTEN

Some companies are completely focused on internal issues and do not find customer feedback valuable. There is no feedback loop and no action in response to the data, because of course there is no data.

FANS OF THE WILD WEST

Finally, there are 'Wild West' companies where there is no data coming in, but new initiatives are launched nonstop. These companies have the stated intention of helping the customer, but there are no customers waiting for the new products. These companies just do … whatever. A few 'Wild West' companies employ brilliant people that have the natural talent to do the right thing without feedback from the market, but these are the exception rather than the rule.

Most readers are probably working in a rough diamond environment. The upside is: the feedback loop may already be installed. The challenge? How to organise to take action faster. If you succeed in this, customer satisfaction will increase, and a positive feedback loop will develop. If customers sense that a company is responding to their request by at least looking for a solution, their motivation to share feedback will increase. This stimulates a positive flow through the feedback loop. More and better customer data leads to more and better decisions.

If you don't know how to start a positive flow, my advice is: copy paste the concept from The Palm. Develop your own customer experience ritual, adjusted to your own feedback loop. Make sure you talk about customer feedback at regular intervals with the people capable of coordinating the action. This occurs daily at The Palm. The regularity of the meeting is up to you. If you have an NPS tracker, useful new data comes in every week. A meeting schedule could be built around the receipt of the NPS tracker data.

HERTZ PUTS CUSTOMERS IN JAIL

I must share an anecdote. It shows what can happen in extreme situations if there is not a proper feedback loop in place and/or the appropriate action is not taken. You are on a road trip across the United States, driving swiftly from national park to national park. Road trip music is blasting through the speakers of your Hertz rental car. The end of the holiday is looming, but you are enjoying yourselves so much that you decide to extend the trip by another five days or so. You book a nice place to stay, reschedule your flight and inform Hertz that you would like to extend your contract. Everything is confirmed and you carry on with the trip. You are en route between the Grand Canyon and Zion National Park when you spot a flashing blue light in your rear-view mirror. Being a sensible driver, you slow down and move aside so that the police can pass smoothly. Suddenly you hear words you do not want to hear: *'Pull over! Pull over! NOW!'* You stop the car on the shoulder of the road, and two highway patrolmen approach your car with their guns drawn. *'Get out of the car and keep your hands where I can see them!'* Minutes later you are handcuffed and sitting in the back of the police car. You are delivered to a police cell.

What was the cause of this dramatic story? A lack of feedback loops at Hertz. To be specific, there was a bug in their software. Although the customers had extended their rental period, when the car was not returned as originally contracted, the car was automatically recorded as stolen. A total of 364 Hertz customers were arrested for this reason. One person spent almost 30 days in jail. In total, Hertz's error resulted in the payment of USD 168 million in damages. How could this have been possible? One would think that after only one false arrest, Hertz would have made it a company-wide priority to solve the problem. Slow feedback loops were probably the cause of the delay.[61]

THE PERFUME OF PETROL VERSUS THE CALIFORNIA SUSHI ROLL

In 2021, Ford conducted a market survey on attitudes towards electric cars. Tesla was the best-known brand and traditional carmakers were slowly starting to enter the market. Ford wanted to define the market entry drivers and barriers for customers to make the switch to electric vehicles. They found that one of the main barriers was the smell of the vehicle. Seventy percent of consumers said they would miss the smell of petrol if they switched to an electric car. The people at Ford decided to address this barrier by creating a perfume that smells like petrol. **My instinct is that consumer feedback may have been taken a little too literally in this case.**[62]

How well do you listen to customer feedback? **Truly listening to customers is a quality of polished diamond companies.** The rumour is that a Ford employee once said: *'If Ford had asked customers what they wanted, they would have replied: faster horses!'* This quote is used by many people who have no interest in customer opinion. Regardless of who uttered these words, they were correct. Polished diamond companies listen to customer feedback, but do not automatically implement it to the letter. The trick is to hear what the customer is really looking for and respond wisely. Our job is not to do what the customer says, our job is to understand what the customer really needs.

Japanese chef Ichiro Mashita ran a sushi restaurant in Los Angeles in the 1960s and 1970s. The restaurant was not a great success. At that time sushi was mostly associated with raw fish, which was not very appealing to the average American consumer. Chef Mashita had two choices: accept that sushi would never appeal to the local population or find a way to adapt raw fish to their food preferences. Chef Mashita chose the second option and began to adapt his sushi recipes. Raw tuna was replaced by avocado, an ingredient that has a certain oiliness like fish. Oiliness is an important quality of tasty sushi. To this he added cooked crab and cucumber, two very popular Californian ingredients. Finally, he decided to transform his new concoction into an 'inside-out' sushi roll, with rice on the outside and the rest of the ingredients on the inside. Today, Chef Mashita's inside out roll is on the menu of almost every sushi restaurant in the United States where the recipe is now known as the California roll.

If Chef Mashita had asked people what they wanted, it is probable that they would have asked for fried fish. He listened to them and fulfilled their wishes by creating a cooked seafood dish but in a way that was connected to his core menu and resulted in success.

Polished diamonds can really listen, which is a fundamental part of putting 'effective empathy' into practice.

MAKE DECISIONS IN PACKED FOOTBALL STADIUMS

I watched every televised Club Brugge football match during the pandemic. I sat at home on our sofa and watched the players do their best in chilly, empty stadiums. The energy was different in those matches from what I was accustomed to, and I found it terrible to watch. Supporters are not meant to hear what the players say and shout to each other. I would have preferred to have heard the supporters singing.

Those conditions must have been terrible for the players as well. A football player can be likened to someone who works in a world of 'real time direct customer feedback'. If they are playing well there is lots of applause. If they commit a foul, they are blanketed in boos. If they score, an explosion of positive emotion is sent in their direction.

What it would be like if you wore an earphone at work that gave you instant, real time, direct, customer feedback on your every decision and action? Imagine: you are writing an email to a customer; you write something that is not very helpful, and you immediately hear booing in your ear. Would you adjust your behaviour? Or imagine that you are behaving in a very customer-focused manner, and you hear cheering. Would you quickly repeat that behaviour?

real time customer feedback

Direct and rapid customer feedback tends to increase customer-centricity. Readers will probably know one of the major problems with customer feedback: too many companies make decisions in empty stadiums. When an important decision is required, excel spreadsheets and PowerPoint files are churned out. The calculations and data these contain are used to form hypotheses and opinions. This ceremony ultimately leads to a decision. Do not misunderstand. I am not data-phobic, nor do I oppose financial analysis. Not at all. They are crucial for making the right decisions in a boardroom. My point is: if you only use data and financial analysis, you dehumanise your customer; they are reduced to a number. The human component must be included in your decision-making process to achieve effective empathy.

The more people in your company are directly confronted with the customer's signs of dismay and delight, the more likely effective empathy will be. 'Hearsay' feedback is not the same as direct feedback.

I would like to share another football analogy with you. I was in the stands for the October 2021 Club Brugge – Paris Saint Germain (PSG) FC All UEFA Champions League match. It was an historic moment for football because it was the first European match with Lionel Messi playing for PSG, having just left FC Barcelona. The world's sporting press had descended on Bruges. Everyone assumed that the star team of Paris – led by Messi – would wipe the floor with Club Brugge. The score was soon 0-1 for PSG. It is the beginning of the end, everyone thought, including me. How wrong we were. Bruges quickly scored an equaliser. Heroic attempts from both teams followed but the match ended at 1-1. However, a tie was seen as a victory in Bruges. Everyone was over the moon and the atmosphere was exuberant. When I got home, my wife, Evi, was watching TV but she had no idea how the match had ended. She asked, *'How was it?'* *'Super,'* I replied enthusiastically, *'We played a draw against Messi and his friends.'* *'I'm happy for you,'* she said as she zapped to a different channel.

We only feel the true impact of an event when we experience it personally. A description of an emotional response is simply that and the feelings are diminished. This is true for customer feedback. If you hear positive or negative feedback directly from the source, it carries more impact than if your read about it through a market research report or hear about it through a colleague's story.

Polished Diamonds have various ways of sharing customer feedback with as many employees as possible. Their matches are all played in packed stadiums.

ARE YOU GOOD AT SAYING 'NO' IN A FRIENDLY WAY?

Remember the daily customer experience meetings at Atlantis The Palm in Dubai? In summary, The Palm categorises customers' questions into frequent questions that need an agreed and consistent response and infrequent questions that may need an individualised or tailored response. You may have read this section quickly. If so, it merits refreshing your memory, because it is an extraordinary and, in my experience, an effective approach. (See Chapter 5)

Many companies have become good at saying 'no' in a friendly way. *'My apologies, Madam, but although we have received your enquiry, we are unable to help you.'* Or *'We apologise for the inconvenience, Sir, but our policies do not permit us to offer assistance on that matter.'*

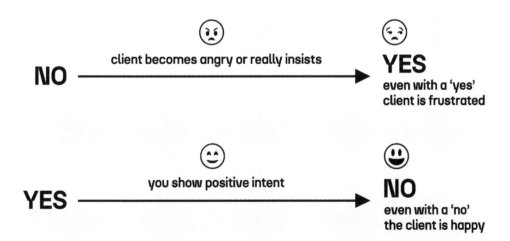

When a somewhat unusual question comes in, the default sentiment too often appears to be, 'Oy, we've never done that for a customer. Just ignore the request.' Persistent customers may be able to convert, a 'no' into a 'yes'. Nonetheless, if customers are made to feel that their question was awkward, difficult to respond to, or required a lot of effort on their behalf, the customer experience overall may still be negative.

What if a company were to take every question seriously? What would be the outcome if a company were to start with a 'yes' by default and if they are unable to respond satisfactorily to the customer's request the answer could become a 'no'? If the customer senses a company's intention to find solutions for its customers, a 'yes' and a 'no' can leave a positive impression.

Some months ago, a group of friends came to visit. We wanted to organise a Spanish evening for them. We planned sangria as an aperitif, tapas to share as starters and paella as a main course. I love to cook and really enjoyed preparing this menu for our guests. The only thing I am not good at and do not like to do is to prepare desserts. But we wanted to round off the Spanish evening with a Spanish dessert. I wanted to serve crema Catalan. A nearby patisserie, Painture, is known for its fine pastries, tasty breads and delicious eclairs. The team there is led by a very good pastry chef. Baker Brecht was Chef Patisserie at the three-star restaurant De Karmeliet in Bruges and his wife Liesbet was the sommelier there. I called them to ask about crema Catalan. *'That's something we have never made before,'* Liesbet told me. *'But I'll ask Brecht what he thinks.'* I could hear her ask Brecht the question. It took less than a second before I heard him answer in the distance. *'Yes, tell him it's fine, I'll take care of it!'*
This may seem like something simple, but it is a prime example of a polished diamond in action: helping the customer without hesitation.

Do you recognise this feeling? If you have a question for a company that is a bit out of the ordinary, you might presume that it could be difficult for the company to respond. **You are, as it were, prepared to hear a 'no'. Then, if you get an immediate 'yes', you are in seventh heaven as a customer.**

When I talk about this philosophy, I regularly get two questions:
1. What if everyone starts asking the same question? The answer is simple. If every customer asks for something, that means it offers value for many customers. An obvious solution is to add the answer to this question to your daily way of working.
2. Surely it is not feasible to say 'yes' to everything? Of course not. My message is not to say 'yes' to everything. My message is, 'Take every question seriously and try to show positive intention.' If you say 'no' to 75% of unexpected customer queries today, that can evolve to 50% by starting with 'yes'. That offers a world of difference for your customers.

THE 'OPEN DOOR BUTTON' HERO!

I like to introduce the 'Say yes more often' mindset to companies by using the 'Open door button' hero analogy. I first read about this concept in an article written by Mitchell Clark.[63] The following is an analogy that explains the concept you have probably experienced yourself: You are alone in a lift. The doors are slowly closing. You enjoy the peace of being alone in the lift. Through the ever-narrowing distance between the two doors, you notice someone rushing towards the lift.
At that moment, you have a choice!

You can press the 'close door' button. 'No luck today, buddy,' you think to yourself just as the doors close and you enjoy the lift in peace. Alternatively, you could become the hero of the moment and press the 'open door' button. Gallantly, you could then hold your arm in front of the door's sensor and kindly say *'Please come in, Madam. Which floor do you wish?'*
Each time you are in an elevator, you have this choice! The same is true for customer questions. You always have a choice!

My favourite place to look for the 'open door' button heroes is at airport security. Next time you are in line there, stop looking at your telephone and look instead for security people holding the door open or just slamming it shut. Some time ago I was headed home from a lecture in Bangkok, flying back to Brussels via Munich. My first flight had landed late in Munich and my next flight to Brussels was already boarding when I disembarked from the Bangkok flight. I was changing from an international to a domestic flight, so I needed to pass again through security. My spirits dropped when I saw the long queue at security. I explained my dilemma to one of the security guards, hoping it might be possible for me to bypass the line and move through security quickly. My question had the opposite effect. The security guard did everything he could to delay my passage through security. I cannot remember ever being checked so thoroughly at Munich. That man pushed the 'close door' button as hard as he could. And he did so in a very successful way. The plane to Brussels left without me on board.

A few weeks later, I was at London's St Pancras Station to catch the Eurostar train home. I arrived at the station a little late. When I saw the long queue at passport control, I knew immediately that I would not make the train. I was about to message my wife to let her know that I would take a later train, when an eager security guard jumped in front of the long queue and shouted, *'Anyone with tickets for the Eurostar to Brussels leaving in about five minutes?'* About five people – including me – raised their hands. *'Everyone else, please take one step to the left!'* It was a magical moment. All those people queuing for other trains were making way for us. It was like Moses parting the Red Sea. I felt like an astronaut coming back from the moon. As I passed a conductor he called out, *'We'll get you on that train, Sir!'* A few minutes later, I was on the train. I arrived home in time for dinner with my family. This is a typical example of an 'open door' button hero! He had the choice and made the right one. This is how polished diamonds reason.

PARTNER IN LIFE!

Effective empathy ultimately leads to a partner in life mindset. A polished diamond's ambition goes beyond purely selling products or services. A polished diamond wants to create positive change in customers' lives in an empathetic way.

In my book *The Offer You Can't Refuse*, I first introduced the concept of 'partner in life'. Of all the ideas and concepts in this book, 'partner in life' created the most new customer strategies in the market. I saw real estate companies become partners in life, every bank and insurer wants to be a partner in life, and B2B companies realise that it is no longer just about their products, but about solving their customers' challenges.

Partner in life is the ultimate form of empathy. You realise the importance of the human within the customer. Every person has a film of their life in her or his head. That film contains their dreams, fears, ambitions and desires. The better you understand the importance of that film of life, the greater the added value you bring to your relationships with customers. A partner in life goes beyond optimising the transactional customer relationship; a partner in life wants an emotional connection with the customer.

To succeed in the partner-in-life strategy, there needs to be a continuous movement. This consists of three steps:

1. Excellent understanding of the needs and frustrations in the customer's life. (Effective empathy)
2. Describing in detail the customer's life journey.
3. Implementing partner-in-life actions.

This is a movement where you translate insights into a concrete description of the customer's life and then take concrete actions. Those actions lead to new behaviour in customers, which in turn leads to new insights, so you keep refining the partner-in-life philosophy. The faster and more effectively you can complete that circle of feedback and action over and over again. in your company, the more you can differentiate yourself from other companies in your sector. In customer experience, there is a very big focus on optimising customer journeys (which is very important), but here we are really looking at the customer's life journey. **The table below clearly summarises the differences between customer and life journeys.**

Customer Journey	Life Journey
Understanding how the customer buys or uses products.	Understanding what dreams, ambitions and fears consumers have in daily life.
Removing frictions in the purchase and service process.	Remove frictions and add value in the customer's daily life.
Mapping customer journey.	Mapping life stages and moments.
Analysis of a company's touchpoints.	Analysis of key moments over a day or over the customer's life.
Transactional optimisation.	Emotional optimisation.

Polished diamonds are a partner in life thanks to their effective empathy.

A PARTNER IN THE SUCCESSFUL LAUNCH OF A CAREER

Most landlords of student lodging have only one goal: to achieve as much return per square metre as possible. Upgrade Estate, the market leader in renting out student lodging in Belgium, wants more. Of course, they want to make a good return, but they also want to help students have a successful start to their lives and careers; they want to be a partner in life for their student clients.

Nele Van Damme and Koenraad Belsack are the founders and joint-CEOs of Upgrade Estate. Their first joint business was a sandwich stall during festivals in the Belgian city of Ghent. They used money made through this collaboration to buy their first building of student lodgings. More than a decade later, they have built student lodgings in Belgium's major university cities. They are backed by a community of investors who believe in their projects. Their buildings and student accommodations are beautifully designed and are fitted with state-of-the-art facilities like fully kitted kitchens and chill-out rooms. They see this as the minimum required to create physically and emotionally positive environments for students. Upgrade Estates makes a difference in the lives of young people with their version of the 'partner in life' philosophy.

Upgrade Estates act on research showing that if a student feels emotionally supported and is in a supportive environment, their chance of success rises. For example, a coach who is committed to the mental wellbeing of the students is available in every building. Coaches offer a supportive environment and help with the practical aspects of life. Upgrade Estates accommodation reflects research showing that if a student is mentally healthy, they have the best chance of success. If a student is dealing with a conflict, or anxiety before exams, or loneliness, or in the worst-case scenario, if someone dies in the building, a coach is there to offer support.

Student residents in Upgrade Estate's accommodation have access to the 'Upgrade Academy' where they can elect to take free courses almost every night of the week. Courses are quite distinct from university topics, such as driving test theory, investing in crypto, how to apply for a job... all are courses that reflect the ethos of Upgrade Estates: to help students start their careers as successfully as possible.

Nele and Koenraad are two very empathetic people. During the pandemic, they sensed the toll it was taking on students' wellbeing. A survey showed that over half of all students reported some level of mental strain. They immediately decided to tap into a group of psychologists and make them available to their students. Every student could book free sessions with the psychologists. **This is a powerful example of effective empathy in action: the feedback loop provided an insight that was immediately transformed into an action.** Upgrade Estates have helped increase the mental strength of their clients and increased the chances that the students' time at university will be a stepping-stone to a successful career.

EFFECTIVE EMPATHY SEEMS LIKE QUITE A STEP FOR MY BUSINESS, STEVEN. WHERE DO WE START?

Introducing effective empathy into your business is a difficult process. It is perhaps the most difficult aspect of transforming a rough diamond into a polished diamond. My advice is very simple: start by exposing as many of your company's employees as possible to direct customer feedback. Get as many people as possible to hear positive and negative feedback directly from customers. This feedback is the beginning of feelings of empathy towards customers throughout your organisation.

It is also important to set up a feedback loop. Build a system through which you receive feedback from customers at very regular intervals. Make sure this feedback is bite sized, i.e., small, easy to read and digest customer insights and quotes. Provide simple summaries of feedback to be shared with as many people as possible.

Finally, you must develop an action-oriented mentality. Select groups of feedback that are easiest to respond to quickly and take the appropriate action. That way, your customers and employees will quickly feel the positive vibes that arise from customer feedback followed by an action (ideally the action will be a solution to a customer's need. Finally, look for a rhythm and structure within your company to incorporate continuous improvement actions into company processes based on customer feedback. These improvement actions should not degenerate into large, complex projects. Focus on making many small improvements in the short term to realise the greatest impact in the long term.

CONCRETE CUSTOMER EXPERIENCE TIPS FROM THIS CHAPTER:

1. Provide a fast feedback system.
2. Create a feedback system that requires little effort from the customer, but provides enough info to you (e.g., Ask for NPS and one open field with the 'why?' question).
3. Provide fast action based on customer feedback: solve the simplest issues first.
4. Share customer feedback with as many employees as possible in a quick and easy format.
5. Have every employee interact with real customers once every six months, Face-to-Face.
6. Organise breakfast meetings with customers to get feedback and make sure someone from a different team is there each time to get that feedback directly.
7. Start with 'Yes'. When a customer question comes in, show positive intent.
8. A customer experience strategy should be felt throughout the company, not just at C-level. Each individual employee needs to understand their role in the larger CX whole, down to what the exact impact would be if they did their job slightly differently.
9. Customer experience strategies begin with your talent strategy. Hire people with the right attitude: those who get genuinely excited about service and who want to give your customers great memories.
10. Empathy needs to be organised as a company and structurally integrated into your business processes.
11. Give your team the chance to become 'open door' heroes (you know, holding that 'open door' button of a lift to help someone altruistically); allow them to break the rules in exceptional situations to help customers in difficult situations. That not only makes the customer feel good but also your staff.
12. Try to find out what your customers are most concerned about and try to help them with that.

CHAPTER 7

WHEN DIGITAL BECOMES HUMAN

'TECHNOLOGY IS NOTHING. WHAT'S IMPORTANT IS THAT YOU HAVE FAITH IN PEOPLE, THAT THEY'RE BASICALLY GOOD AND SMART, AND IF YOU GIVE THEM TOOLS, **THEY'LL DO WONDERFUL THINGS WITH THEM'**

STEVE JOBS

THE CHINESE ALGORITHMS

Temu, an e-commerce app that is part of the Chinese conglomerate, Pinduoduo, had more downloads in the United States than companies like Amazon and Walmart during Q2 22.[64] Almost anything can be purchased on the Temu app, from clothes to shoes to electronics. If you download the app, you immediately notice the preponderance of low priced products. Through very aggressive marketing – even advertising during the Super

Bowl – they attract many people to their platform, where they are seduced by the enormous range of very low priced items. Like the very popular Chinese fashion platform Shein, Temu ships products directly from the factory to the customer. This saves a lot of costs on department stores and logistics, allowing them to price their products much lower than traditional retailers.

Another driver of their success is artificial intelligence. As you use the Temu app, its algorithm profiles you very quickly. It remembers which products you look at longer than others, what you click on and for which items you seek additional information. In less than half an hour, the system gets to know you and begins to show you more and more products that fit your search profile. This flow of products chosen within an individual's sphere of interest, at very low prices, is addictive for many people.

In this sense, the Temu algorithm is very similar to the Shein and TikTok algorithms. At Shein (which is now bigger than H&M and Zara in terms of turnover), you are constantly shown new clothes that the AI knows you like. The clothes are virtually designed to suit your taste. Shein also has no problem producing clothes in small quantities, so you get a very strong form of personalisation. Their production works completely in reverse to that of a classic fashion house. In the classic process, a designer designs the clothes, then the clothes go to the shop where the consumer buys them. At Shein, it looks at what people click on and throw in their shopping basket, and it is only then that the clothing is produced. This means that the data and the consumer decide essentially on what is produced.

A characteristic of these three companies is the high efficiency of their algorithms. In a very short time, each system comes to know you very well, and begins to constantly feed you content that is within your interests with the result that many people also become addicted to these platforms. Of course, these companies are heavily criticised for their methods. Luring young people to become addicted to a social network is not ideal for their futures. Fashion producers like Shein and Temu are pushing the consumer society in a direction we just should not go in if we want to keep the climate somewhat under control.

My objective for this book is to explore what we can learn from this technology, and not to focus on its social impact. TikTok's main factor for success is undoubtedly its interface: it is fast, easy, entertaining and informative. In my opinion, these are the characteristics of the interface of the future. Most of our existing technology lacks these characteristics. For example, consider Google's search engine. When you enter a question, you get millions of links and need to search within these for the response that best suits your interests. Of course, over the years Google has found ways to consolidate and prioritise search results but output remains a long list of links. The same happens if you search for a house to buy or a hotel to book; the output is an endless list of options. A comparison of Google and TikTok's interfaces reveals the latter's superiority.

Technology today makes it possible to create fast, easy to use, entertaining and educational interfaces. Amazon, meanwhile, is experimenting with a TikTok-style interface to introduce products to its customers. Spotify is working with an AI DJ that selects music for users and bridges the selections if desired. Why would companies not 'TikTok' their interfaces or at least consider the possibilities?

IT'S HARD WITHOUT AI: CHATGPT CAN MAKE YOUR CUSTOMER EXPERIENCE MORE EFFICIENT

December 2022 and Q1 2023 will go down in history as a landmark year. Just as 2007 went down in history as the start of the mobile era (thanks to the arrival of the iPhone), 2023 will be the start of the real era of artificial intelligence. The arrival of ChatGPT plus its integration into search engines and Microsoft office is a change of era. **Numerous companies, meanwhile, are already using ChatGPT to make their customer experience more productive.**

ChatGPT can enhance customer experience in 5 ways:

1. *New generation chatbots.* Most customer service chatbots have a supporting script on which the conversation with the customer is based. Think of it as a very large answer tree from which the software can choose. ChatGPT-based chatbots will be much more 'conversational'. It is like having a conversation with a human: the quality of answers is much better, you can ask further questions after an answer. If the quality of ChatGPT can be used by default in customer service chatbots, we will experience a breakthrough in automated customer service.

2. *Intelligence Augmented.* Customers' queries can be passed to ChatGPT by customer service agents. The chatbot's answer can then be slightly modified as needed by an employee before it goes to the customer. If, for example, an e-mail needs to be composed and sent to several customers to advise that a product is out of stock, ChatGPT can draft the e-mail and an employee can finish it and forward it to the customers. The amount of time that the employee will be occupied by such tasks will be reduced by at least 50%, a significant increase in employee productivity.

3. *Conversation Management.* Companies often receive consumer requests via social media that must be answered by human employees one by one, a labour intensive process. Suppose you could use AI to respond to reviews on Tripadvisor or OpenTable, for example. This could lead to an increase in the number of responses per human employee.

4. *Creative ideas.* It can be difficult to come up with ideas for something fun to offer customers. A solution might be to organise a brainstorming session with colleagues. Alternatively, you might brief ChatGPT, resulting in an infinite source of new ideas, some of which your team would not have come up with on their own. From those, you might select a few to leave with your team to develop further. ChatGPT can be a boost to your creativity; like a free consultant.

5. *Faster development of interfaces.* Companies regularly receive customers' critiques, often justified, on the functioning of their app or website. Addressing those critiques can be problematic. The customer experience team may need help from the IT team to make a small adjustment to the site. IT teams' schedules are almost always booked well in advance, so it might take months before even minor adjustments are visible to customers. What if your ChatGPT could modify the code? The AI bot can code and can customise code which might allow you to make certain adjustments in a matter of minutes. With faster interface adjustments, you will get more satisfied customers.

THE NEW GATEKEEPER

Over the past few years, I had the pleasure of working occasionally with Benedict Evans, in my opinion one of the best technology analysts you can find. His weekly newsletter has almost 200.000 subscribers and I highly recommend signing up for it. For just a few minutes of your time, you will have weekly insights into what is happening in the world of technology. Every year, he also creates a new keynote presentation in which he shares his latest insights. His presentations usually consist of about 100 slides of charts and statistics, from which Benedict builds a story.

The theme of his January 2023 presentation was the new gatekeepers.[65] Years ago, US department stores were the gatekeepers for products. In the 1980s, these chains realised about 30% of all retail sales in the US. At the time of writing in 2023, that figure had dwindled to less than five percent. Newspapers were long the gatekeepers of information. Almost 80% of all advertising budgets went to newspapers in the 1930s. Today, this figure too has tumbled to less than five percent. In the past, each region had its own newspaper, TV station and radio station so the gatekeepers were regionally organised. Today, the majority of ad budgets go to three companies: Alphabet (Google), Meta (Facebook) and Bytedance (including TikTok). His conclusion is clear. The former gatekeepers (traditional media and distribution) have been replaced by new, global gatekeepers (Amazon, Google, Facebook), but their role too will diminish in terms of impact in the coming years. The cause: artificial intelligence. The quality of AI will continue to improve, encouraging increasing numbers of people to adopt it.

We all know that ChatGPT sometimes makes errors, but given its very high rate of accuracy, hardly anyone checks the system anymore. Imagine what our behaviour will look like when we are another decade away and ChatGPT performance has improved several fold. It is inevitable that slowly but surely, AI will be introduced into our lives. Slowly but surely, we will start relying on it more and more. Before we know it, AI will be the new gatekeeper in our lives. By the way, this is the world I describe in my three Romy Bell thrillers (*Eternal, The Upgrade, High Betrayal*). Romy cannot get through everyday life without her AI assistant, Joanne. My fiction books are set between 2041 and 2048. Something tells me that sooner rather than later our personal AI will be a regular companion, assisting us to make our lives easier and more efficient. **I can confidently tell you that when writing this book, ChatGPT was the best research assistant I have ever had.**

My book *Customers the Day after To-morrow* describes in detail what the impact of AI on customer experience will be. It also covers the story of the new gatekeeper. **What if people ask for advice on products from their AI assistant? Which brands will score well there and which brands will not? The AI assistant becomes the gatekeeper and can therefore decide which brands can pass the filter and which cannot.** Being well informed about gatekeeper management will become part of the customer experience of the (near) future.

THE ADDED VALUE FOR CUSTOMERS OF TECHNOLOGY

Clearly, we are on the eve of a major technological revolution. In the coming months and years, you will be bombarded with AI solution providers. Everything will look super and some will be more impressive than others. Moreover, to become a polished diamond, it will be necessary to keep up with this evolution. Without AI, life could be difficult – more difficult than it needs to be.

When making your decisions regarding the purchase and use of technology, do not get carried away by the trendy nature of the technology and always ask the one crucial question: how can technology create added value for the customer? Most importantly, realise that technology can never be the 'guiding star' of your customer strategy. Every time there is hype around a new technology, new applications emerge that no one is actually waiting for. The result is too many solutions searching for a problem. This benefits no one. The guiding star of a customer strategy should be the customer's needs. Once this is appreciated, you are ready to learn how technology can help you meet the customer's needs.

There are three major benefits for customers if you make smart use of technology.

1. EFFICIENCY

Technology can make customers' (and employees') lives more efficient. Thanks to e-commerce, we no longer have to leave the house when we want to buy something. We can perform our banking transactions with our smartphones so that a visit to a bank branch is not necessary. Checking into a flight electronically in advance can help us avoid the queue at the check-in desk. Navigation apps can help us avoid traffic jams. Rainfall radar apps prevent us from being drenched in a thunderstorm or at least warn us to carry an umbrella. There are a few hundred more examples. Lots of things that used to take up a lot of our time now happen (almost) automatically.

If you have to explain Amazon's success in one word, it is: efficiency! Time is our most precious commodity and Amazon manages to help us save time. The company that saves most of our time is also the company that gets most of our time. Amazon has surely succeeded at this.

Non-technology companies have also sucessfully implemented digital efficiency. The My Disney Experience app, for example, is a useful companion for an efficient visit to Disneyland. Domino's Pizza's success is largely due to their very user-friendly app interface that helps customers (re)order their favourite pizza with virtually zero effort.

2. PERSONALISATION

If anyone else on the planet has the same collection of apps on their iPhone homepage as I do, I would find it very creepy. After all, each of us has curated our own collection of apps and we all have our own manner of organising our apps, right? The chance that two people share precisely the same apps, organised in the same way is virtually non-existent. **Mobile phone technology allows us to create our own world, to get recommendations tailored to a profile and to be notified of promotions when we are near a particular shop.** As described previously, customers like personalisation and it creates greater loyalty. Technology helps us to realise these benefits. It is the most famous example of 'the segment of 1'.

David Vélez is known as the founder of the first truly digital bank, Nubank, Brazil. After years of frustration with traditional Brazilian banks, he decided to do better himself. The new bank was founded in 2013. The bank's first mission was to make banking easy. Proof that the bank accomplished this mission is that its concept has since been copied by other neo-banks worldwide. The bank's current mission is to help their customers save in a personalised way. In September 2022, they launched their 'Caixinhas' (small boxes to save money in) concept. Customers can create boxes to save for certain goals. The boxes will be fully personalised. Customers can name them themselves or attach photos. People immediately started saving for their dream trip to Europe or a new car. A personal savings plan is created for each depositor so they can easily track how long they need to save before reaching their personal goal. The simple, personalised concept was an instant hit. In the first week, 1.7 million customers created 2.25 million Caixinhas.

3. CREATIVITY/ENTERTAINMENT

When I released my book *When Digital Becomes Human* in 2014, the belief was still alive that creativity was a typically human quality. In the meantime, we now know better. Artificial intelligence can paint works of art, compose music scores and create delicious recipes. **AI can be creative and thus add value for customers.**

For example, if you are looking for a unique visual for a presentation, you can now enlist the help of DALL-E. DALL-E generates images based on your written description. That way, you no longer have the same stock images in your slides that everyone else uses. You will then have a unique visual that will make you stand out, thanks to the creativity of an AI system.

Companies with strong customer culture (polished diamonds) manage to bring these three benefits to life thanks to the right investments. Moreover, polished diamonds usually manage to be fast followers in the adoption of new technology. **Customer-centric companies listen to their customers and use that input to** make the right technology choices. **If effective empathy (see previous chapter) works well, then you know what your customers need.** By starting from the customer's need, polished diamonds do not go along with the hype, but invest in tools and software that deliver immediate customer benefits.

SPARKX

I remember it well. During the first weeks of the COVID lockdown, I received a phone call from Mathieu Renier. I knew Mathieu as a passionate employee at sports retailer Decathlon.
'Steven, I have an idea I would like to bounce off you sometime. It has to do with my daughter,' he began to tell me in his enthusiastic style. *'She wants to play sports and not just one sport but several. Sometimes she wants to play tennis, other times it is skating and then it's basketball.'*
'Very familiar, Mathieu, our youngest son is just the same,' was my response.
'You know, I'm glad to hear that. Because I have an idea!'

In the minutes that followed, he told me about his dream to develop an amusement park where everyone – young, old, experienced or inexperienced – could try a wide variety of sports in an interactive way. I was immediately sold on the idea. A few months later, Mathieu quit his job at Decathlon and started building his dream – SparkX. Funded by a group of investors (of which I was very proudly one, contributing a small part), the plans became concrete. During the spring of 2023, the first SparkX park, Europe's largest sports entertainment park, opened in Hasselt (Belgium). Meanwhile, plans are being forged for subsequent locations. The aim is to become a European player with this original concept.

SparkX correlates well with the three benefits digitalisation can bring to customers today:

EFFICIENCY

At SparkX, you can practise or try 50 sports in one location. The simulators, interactive screens and augmented reality applications make it possible to try out many different sports during one visit. For example, there is a sports fishing simulator, a Formula 1 simulator and a clay pigeon shooting game; all sports you cannot decide to do spontaneously when the mood strikes you. More conventional sports such as football, tennis, archery, skiing, climbing... can also be tried at SparkX.

The sports are displayed as realistically as possible, thanks to technology. The technology is not intended to create virtual reality experiences per se, but to simulate to simulate the actual experience of the sport as closely as possible. Without this technology, such a park would not be possible. The SparkX concept ticks the box for efficiency because customers can try a very large number of sports in one location: super-efficient.

PERSONALISATION

On admission to SparkX customers are given a digital bracelet that keeps track of their physical performance data during the visit. Casual visitors to SparkX are interested to learn how they performed and professional athletes can be satisfied too: the digital bracelets can serve as a tracking tool to update their training schedule and monitor their progress.

CREATIVITY

Thanks to SparkX's Formula 1 simulator, you can imagine yourself to be Max Verstappen, the Dutch-Belgian racing driver. Or perhaps paragliding? You may not dare to paraglide off a mountain right away, but you can already try it out in the simulator. SparkX's technology offers a whole new experience to visitors and lowers their barriers to try a sport. Creative solutions create new opportunities.

In a 'real' sports environment, it is sometimes less fun to play when you have players of different levels in the game. The top players get frustrated by the less talented ones. The latter group also have less fun because they feel they cannot handle the level. In SparkX, this level difference is solved by augmented reality. For some players, the challenge is made harder, for others easier. That way, everyone in the group or family can experience sports together in a fun way.

'WE ARE NOT A TECHNOLOGY COMPANY!'

Technology is playing an ever-increasing and important role in customer relations. It is simply no longer possible to become a polished diamond without it. Technology may not be a short cut to more satisfied customers, but not using technology is a short cut to more dissatisfied customers. Because almost every company has become convinced of the role of technology, many companies have begun positioning themselves as technology based. *'Henceforth, we are a mobile first company,'* has become a familiar slogan for years. I have seen it emblazoned across posters on the walls of many companies.

The technology first mindset was accelerated by Marc Andreessen's now famous observation during an interview in 2011 that, 'software is eating the world'.[66] Andreessen, founder of Netscape and currently one of the most influential investors in Silicon Valley, explained in that interview how companies like AirBnB, Uber and Amazon were turning traditional business models on their heads. The capabilities of technology were at the root of that disruption. Suddenly, every company was afraid of being attacked by the 'Uber' of their industry. Company X needs to become the Uber of their industry, was a common statement. It created an unprecedented investment in technology and digital tools.

I had the opportunity to give a presentation to the management of Belgian media company DPG. It was very refreshing to hear Christian Van Thillo (DPG chairman) say just the opposite. 'Dear people, remember it well. I cannot say it more clearly: we are not a technology company. We are a company with a passion for media that also knows how to make excellent use of technology. That technology is necessary, but that is not our passion. Our passion is making news and telling great stories. That is where our strength lies and that is where we should always put as many resources as possible.' Moreover, Christian Van Thillo delivered his admonition in such a wonderfully energetic and charismatic way that it was met with hearty applause. In my opinion, Van Thillo hit the nail on the head. Technology is necessary to meet customer expectations for ease of use, but real success requires passion. That is where you can really make a difference.

Why did companies like Uber become so popular? Because they were more user-friendly than the alternatives. But the times when companies could control a market segment by offering ease of use are now behind us. In my book *The Offer You Can't Refuse*, I explained that digital convenience has become a commodity. It is not special anymore. It is expected and taken for granted: without it, you lose market share. **It is no longer the ticket to the gold medal, it is only the ticket to play along.** Very few companies win customers purely because of technology; companies win customers by displaying their passion.

INTELLIGENCE AUGMENTED

Many people cringe when a new technology emerges, lamenting the job losses that they predict are sure to follow. Sometimes this is true. There are no longer as many horseshoe manufacturers as there were a hundred years ago, but tyre plants have taken their place as a consequence of innovation.

When ChatGPT launched, news of the jobs to be lost ricochetted around the internet. The reality has been somewhat different. Instead, new techologies can lead to the evolution of job descriptions. Over time, the content of our jobs changes. This is fortunate. Imagine you are still doing the same thing you were doing ten years ago in exactly the same way. Worklife would be boring.

Periods of long transformation can lead to the disappearance of old jobs and the appearance of new jobs. Perhaps job transformation is occuring more rapidly than before, but so far no major waves of unemployment have resulted from the implementation of smart technology. In fact, the number of people in work and the need for extra talent is greater than ever. The biggest challenge that many companies face is just finding people to hire, meaning that technology that boosts productivity is in demand. 'Your job won't be taken away by AI, your job will be taken away by someone who can work well with AI,' is a quote that popped up a lot on the internet (I do not know the original source). This is possibly the essence of the labour market of the future.

The future will feature the collaboration between people and artificial intelligence, boosting employee productivity and people scalability. The term 'Intelligence Augmented' describes this way of working. A report by McKinsey calculated that smart use of AI combined with human capability could give rise to an increase in economic activity of USD 13 trillion by 2030.[67] We will see this approach in just about every industry in the coming years. An example is JP Morgan's AI COIN (contract intelligence) system for the analysis of complex legal documents. Thanks to AI, human effort is drastically reduced and the likelihood of faulty analysis decreases and, in this example, the risk of implementing contracts with unintended loopholes decreases. In 2030, will you still believe a diagnosis from a doctor who does not use an AI assistant? Would and should it still be justified for a radiologist make conclusions based solely on the interpretation of data by only humans?

When I had the opportunity to work with the paint industry federation a few months ago, I was amazed at the potential of intelligence augmentation in that industry. There are two main branches in the paint industry: making buildings more beautiful and making certain products and installations safer (e.g. the paint on an Airbus or a pipeline in the ocean).

intelligence augmented

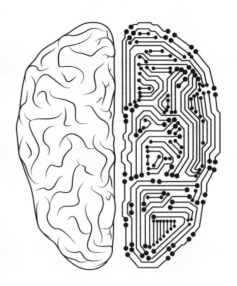

Artificial intelligence is used in both branches to increase productivity. In making a building more beautiful, the choice of colour is a very important factor. Artificial intelligence works as a consultant together with the specialists. I tried it myself using ChatGPT. I described our living room as accurately as possible: the surface area, the impact of natural light, the wooden floor, the colour of the furniture and a description of what hangs on the wall. The chatbot generated four suggestions, each was discussed and argued in a clear way. Then I asked the AI system for its favourite. The answer was an exact match with what an interior designer had recommended to us a few years ago and with the colour walls are actually painted. The next step was to upload a picture of our room to visualise the effect in 2D and 3D. A tool like ChatGPT could serve as a research team to help formulate advice or double-check ideas.

AI is being used with increasing frequency on the technical side of the paint industry. There is a scarcity of skilled painters in the market, so the need for automation is becoming great. AI has become a routine tool for painting large ships in China and AI has assisted in the selection of paint used to protect undersea pipelines. In my opinion, all industries will use AI in the future to meet new standards of productivity.

THE NEW SKILLSET

I met Vincent Bragg and Joe Nickson on an inspiration trip to Los Angeles. They are the founders of the advertising agency ConCreates. Before founding ConCreates, they were both inmates at a US federal prison. Vincent had run a successful drug empire with revenues of USD 350 million a year. Joe, only 23 when we met, had (allegedly, Joe specifies) already pulled off 22 successful bank robberies. When they were released from prison they started their own advertising agency. They believe that successful criminals must be more creative than entrepreneurs. They offer their creativity to the market. Everyone who works in their company is an ex-convict.

As we spoke, I became captivated by their 'transferable skills' mindset. Vincent put it like this: 'I wasn't a drug dealer, I was an expert in logistics!' Joe added, 'Anyone can rob a bank. The trick is being creative enough to know how to get away with it. Hence, I am now creative director of our agency.'

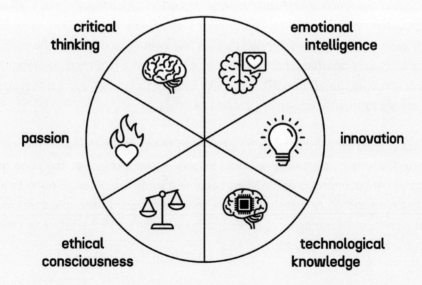

Regardless of whether you are a fan of their story or not, the concept of trans-ferable skills is super interesting. It is about skills you can transfer to different roles, talents that will gain importance in any job. Each of us will have to iden-tify, develop and promote our talents to add value in this new world of work.

The following skills are becoming increasingly important and will add value in any 'intelligence augmented' job:

1. *Critical thinking and problem-solving skills.* Talent to take the computer's delivered work to the next level. Not all computer output is suitable to use or to send to a customer right away. Vincent Bragg, co-founder and CEO of ConCreates, summed it up when he said: 'In school, you learn to read, but not how to read between the lines. Let that be just the skill you need most in these modern times.'

2. *Emotional intelligence.* Computers excel in data analysis, but have no un-derstanding of emotions and social nuances. Emotional intelligence is nec-essary to understand the human aspects of a situation and respond em-pathically.

3. *Passion.* Computers have no passion. Artificial intelligence does not get ex-cited by positive customer feedback, humans do. Coming across as passion-ate and enthusiastic to the customer therefore is especially valuable (in combination with the Top Gun Effect; Chapter 2).

4. *Innovation.* AI can serve as a perfect source of inspiration for new ideas. I know of advertising agencies that first ask ChatGPT for input when they need to come up with a new brand name, for example. The AI input speeds up brainstorming. Humans use the computer output to build on.

5. *Ethical consciousness.* AI has no consciousness; it does not think. Humans need to apply their ability to make correct ethical choices when interpreting AI advice.

6. *Technological knowledge.* There is no need for everyone to become an AI expert, but a basic understanding of how AI works and how to work with it is becoming increasingly important. We will increasingly have to deal with AI in our private and professional lives. The better we can deal with it, the better our chances of being more productive in life.

WHEN DIGITAL BECOMES HUMAN

My book *When Digital Becomes Human* was published in 2014. Currently, I find the topic of this book – How to combine technological interfaces with human qualities to best help customers – more topical than ever. That is also why I chose *When Digital Becomes Human* as the title of this chapter. We are at the start of a new big wave of technology (AI) that may be even more impactful than the advent of the internet and the iPhone. It will fundamentally change the way we work, the way we communicate with customers and how we will help customers. More than ever, there is a need to prepare for a double trans-formation. Indeed, to become a polished diamond, you face a double challenge as a company:

♦ **The digital transformation.** Learn to use technology to generate value for cus-tomers in efficiency, personalisation, creativity.
♦ **The human transformation**. Change the skillset of your employees so that they bring lasting value in an intelligence augmented world.

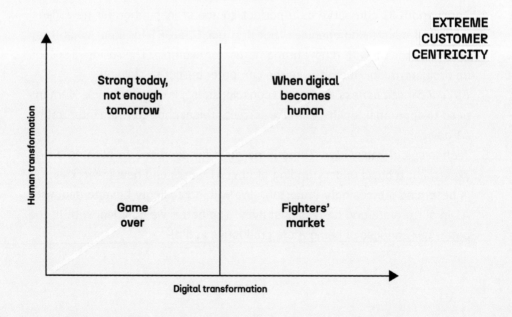

SparkX aims to capitalise on the three customer technology benefits (digital transformation, see page 5), but their business model adds additional benefits by bringing a human component to the story. SparkX dreams of increasing their customers' wellbeing both physically, through exercise and a choice of healthy food in the park, and mentally, through school workshops, yoga sessions. It is a technological story strongly supported by a human component. This was also Christian Van Thillo's message: we make the difference because of our passion (our humanity); we also excel in technology. (see page 8). If we manage to combine the strengths of the human with the strengths of the technological, we reach the point 'when digital becomes human'.

In March 2023, Bill Gates published an article entitled *The Age of AI has Begun*.[68] He considered the strength of ChatGPT as the second most impressive moment of his career. The first moment was the introduction of the graphical computer interface, which later led to the development of Windows. This innovation made computing accessible to everyone. Today, he sees ChatGPT as the innovation that makes AI accessible to all. According to Gates, one of the most important consequences is that humanity will finally have time to perform really important human tasks: education, caring for lonely people, caring for patients... I love that tech optimism. Who knows, maybe the *When Digital Becomes Human* era will dawn within a few decades.

DARE TO BE TRULY HUMAN

The importance of being purely human has not diminished in the digital world. People have a unique talent to pass energy to one another. This was evident during the COVID lockdowns. I received more invitations to present on my topics of expertise than ever before. Of course, they were all digital presentations. I was particularly grateful that I could continue working, but, in all honesty, it required a lot of energy from me. When presenting by video you must project a lot of energy through the screen to have impact, but little energy was returned during the COVID lockdown period. It was only then that I realised the impact of human energy. When you stand in a room (even if there are only 10 people) you always get energy back. That give and take between people is a source of strength. Online technology events and meetings may be very efficient, but they are ineffective for exchanging energy with other people and making connections with them.

People rarely become big fans of companies that are only digital. Perhaps you are thinking that Amazon discredits this statement. You are correct; many people are mega fans of Amazon even if they have never spoken personally with anyone at the company. In case of dire need, you can make phone contact with someone at Amazon and if you have, you will have found it a very pleasant experience. The reality is: there are not that many Amazons in the world. Most companies need only pure humanity to win a customer's heart.

Given the rate of acceleration in the quality of artificial intelligence, I am sure many companies are already dreaming of a fully automated customer service department. Within a number of years, it will probably be perfectly possible. The question is: would it be a good thing? How would customers be affected: no more hanging on the line listening to music, no more of those annoying menus that never offer a number corresponding to your need, no more voice with a heavy accent that makes their words incomprehensible. Would customers find this appealing? I am convinced that 95% of the time, they would. If something is wrong with their internet, or they want to rebook a flight, or they have a very practical question about a product, AI customer service is without a doubt the best solution. Suppose your house has burned down, you have had a bad accident or someone has died unexpectedly, you might prefer to speak with a real human being, who empathises with your situation and takes some time to do so. Polished diamonds will never completely remove the human component, even if it is technologically possible. Polished diamonds provide either efficiency or the human touch as appropriate.

In an effort to confront loneliness by facilitating human contact, Dutch supermarket chain Jumbo has installed over 200 'chat checkouts' since 2022. People who opt for the 'chat checkout' can talk with the cashier for 15 to 30 minutes without anyone making a fuss. Customers who are in a rush can opt for other checkout lanes.

Southwest Airlines' customer service strategy also includes a human option. Customers can choose to arrange everything concerning their flights digitally, but once on board the airline has found a clever way to make use of the time the customer is physically present. Few companies have the luxury of their customers being 'captive' with company representatives with them for several hours. There is no alternative. Most airlines treat this unique moment as transactional, promoting duty free products, meals, snacks and drinks, while Southwest has chosen to make time on board fun and entertaining for customers. With a search on YouTube, you will find videos of the Southwest crews joking, or singing through the intercom, sharing their human energy with their customers.

EACH DEPARTMENT HAS TWO RESPONSIBILITIES: THE OPERATIONAL AND THE CULTURAL

We are coming to the end of our diamond polishing process. One important question remains to be answered:

Who can take a leading role in polishing the diamond? All the people who lead a team, in my opinion. My view is that each department has two duties: operational duties and cultural responsibilities. A factory manager obviously must ensure production quality, efficiency and safety. But the manager also has cultural responsibilities. If an unexpected customer demand should arise or if a problem develops that threatens to leave customers feeling dissatisfied, the manager's handling of that problem, including how the team is informed about the problem, is important. Culturally responsible managers will not treat such problems as burdens or brush them off. Instead, they will seek a solution while communicating transparently and proactively. Culturally responsible managers take responsibility. They know to use such events to demonstrate 'can do' attitudes and in doing so they will help to build company culture. Treating unexpected problems as something negative will also build the company culture but not the way you want if your goal is to be a polished diamond.

The same can be said about every executive in your organisation. The human resources director has operational duties, but certainly also cultural ones too. Even the billing department can be viewed in the same way. It can be quite valuable to talk about the two components of a manager's role in the context of brainstorming or strategy meetings. The message: we expect you to do your job well, but we also expect you to help build our customer-centric culture.

CONCRETE CUSTOMER EXPERIENCE TIPS FROM THIS CHAPTER:

1. Experiment as much as possible with new technology. Then think about the customer benefits. Only then make a decision.
2. Provide enough customer reviews and content on the internet so that in a future with AI as gatekeeper, you will be found by the algorithm.
3. Mirror your customers' communication channels. If the customer prefers WhatsApp, then use WhatsApp. If the customer prefers phone, then use the phone.
4. Do the 'click to order' test on your own site. Go to your own website and order your own products. If it is not fast enough, remove the main frictions.
5. Look at your own website via your mobile and surf to each page. Adjust the frictions.
6. Use technology only if it increases employee productivity.
7. Observe which employees naturally combine the most empathy, enthusiasm and efficiency. Let these people interact with your customers as much as possible.
8. Remind every manager in your company that they have both an operational and a cultural responsibility.
9. Remember the 90% – 10% principle with technology, where it works perfectly in the 90% but leaves a lot to be desired in the latter. Make sure your human team addresses that 10% so there is no customer frustration with a sub-optimal digital experience.
10. Do not just use your customers' data to make them smarter themselves. Make them smarter with their own data on their health, shopping behaviour, financial behaviour, etc.

A DIAMOND IN THE ROUGH VERSUS THE POLISHED DIAMOND

We have reached the end of Part 2. You know the difference between rough diamonds and polished diamonds. You have understood the challenges of becoming customer-centric and how to effectively manage it. Part 1 was about brightening the diamond (the Top Gun Effect, your circle of influence and belief) and Part 2 was about transforming the bright diamond into a polished diamond (the customer loyalty flywheel, effective empathy and finally via the *When Digital Becomes Human* philosophy). As discussed at the end of part 1, it is time to pause and take out the *How to Become a Shiny Diamond Workbook* and see what actions you can initiate within your own organisation. Where will you start? What quick wins are there? What are the more challenging projects?

To round off this section, here are some key differences between the rough diamond and the polished diamond.

Rough Diamond	Polished Diamond
Customer loyalty starts with the customer	Customer loyalty starts with our company
Uses classic loyalty programmes	Builds a community of enthusiastic customers
Always expects short-term returns from every customer effort	Does the right thing for the customer without expecting anything in return in the short term
Slow and complex feedback loops	Fast and simple feedback loops
Slow action after customer feedback	Fast action after customer feedback
Maximum efficiency through technology	Combines efficiency with real humanity
Focuses on technology	Focuses on the customer benefits of technology

How do you score on these seven dimensions? Where are you already a polished diamond and where do you exhibit rough diamond behaviour? You can score yourself on each of these dimensions to see where action is required in the workbook. As I wrote in the beginning of this book: it is my dream to see as many polished diamonds as possible appear in the coming years. I wish you all the energy and enthusiasm needed to take action and make this happen.

Our diamond is polished now, but the story is not yet finished. The world in which our polished diamond operates is changing faster than ever. The work is never finished. Polished diamonds understand better than anyone else how to keep up with evolution in the market and to constantly adapt to new realities. In the third and final part of this book, we are going to prepare for continuous adaptation by answering the question:

How can you keep your polished diamond polished in today's 'never normal' society?

CUSTOMER FOCUS IN 'THE NEVER NORMAL'

PART 3: CUSTOMER FOCUS IN 'THE NEVER NORMAL'

Peter Hinssen published his book *The New Normal* in 2010. His book describes how digitalisation has become the new normal. At that time, the term 'digital camera' had been replaced by, simply, 'camera'. Digitalisation became pervasive and became normal for the majority of people. In 2020, the world was beset by the COVID pandemic. In a matter of days, our behaviour changed completely and truly until everything in our lives had a digital component. Digital aperitifs, online meetings, food delivery; the changes seemed interminable. People debated whether the world was reaching a tipping point. The post-COVID era would be nothing like the pre-COVID era. As I write this in March 2023, the corona virus lockdowns seem like something from the distant past. The reality is that we do not live today as we did during the lockdowns. Some things are back to square one. In real life (IRL) aperitifs with friends being the most fun, of course. Other things have changed permanently. Working 100% at the office is something most people no longer do as one example. Meanwhile, a war is raging, inflation has exploded and we are increasingly confronted with climate issues.

One thing is clearer than ever: there is no 'new normal'. We are facing more and more shocks and they are succeeding each other faster. Today, we are living in a 'Never Normal'.

In this final part, I want to give you the tools and insights to prepare for the never normal. Radiant diamonds closely follow the latest trends in the market. Radiant diamonds have the flexibility to adapt their plan of action to the ever-changing environment they find themselves in. If you want to remain a radiant diamond, you have no choice but to be mindful of the never normal.

The Never Normal (chapter 8)
In this chapter, I asked Peter Hinssen, the creator of the never normal concept, to share his insights with us. In his well-known style, Peter takes us through the latest important evolutions and how to deal with them as an organisation.

The Never Normal Customer (chapter 9)
With constant changes in the world, you also get changes in terms of consumer behaviour and needs. How to describe the never normal customer and how to deal with it as an organisation.

CHAPTER 8

THE NEVER NORMAL

BY **PETER HINSSEN**, NEXXWORKS CO-FOUNDER, BUSINESS
INNOVATION KEYNOTE SPEAKER, AUTHOR AND LECTURER

It is quietly becoming a fine tradition. This is the third book in which my good friend and business partner Peter Hinssen has written a guest chapter. I am very happy about this. Peter is a successful entrepreneur, an expert in digital technology and an excellent business strategist. Above all, Peter is a very engaging writer and speaker. I highly recommend his books (*The Phoenix and the Unicorn* is his most recent book).

As mentioned previously, Peter shares his views on 'the never normal' in this chapter.

Thanks for your contribution, Peter!

'INTELLIGENCE IS THE *ABILITY TO ADAPT TO CHANGE'*

STEPHEN HAWKING

MAGIC TO NORMAL

Douglas Adams, the author of *The Hitchhiker's Guide to the Galaxy* and one of my all-time favourite writers had an interesting definition of technology: 'Technology is the name we give to things that don't actually work yet.' Perhaps even better is the quote from science-fiction writer Sir Arthur C. Clarke in his book *Profiles of the Future* where he writes: 'Any sufficiently advanced technology is indistinguishable from magic.'

My first mainstream business book, *The New Normal*, was published in 2010. I really loved that title when it came out. But over time I would come to regret my choice. Especially when the term was hijacked during the pandemic and became synonymous with the impact of all things COVID, and the negative elements related to the lockdowns. What I really wanted to address with *The New Normal* was the adoption of digital technology. In fact, I still remember having to explain what 'digital' was, back in the early days of this century.

When the iPhone was introduced in 2007, Steve Jobs told his audience, 'This will be your life in your pocket, the ultimate digital device.' Most of the people sitting in that auditorium had no idea what he was talking about, but just a few years later it would only seem logical, natural and, simply 'normal'.

Digital went from 'magic' to 'mainstream' in a decade.
The adoption of all things digital followed an S-curve, as I described in the book. **In the first half of this curve, digital was 'special', but when the adoption started to rise, it quickly flipped over into the second leg where it became ordinary or 'normal'.** At the time, cameras were the perfect example. Initially we would get excited about a 'digital' camera, and then almost overnight all cameras became digital. An 'old' analogue camera turned into a rarity, a collector's item, and digital cameras became normal. We refer to them as cameras now. The adjective 'digital' has become superfluous.

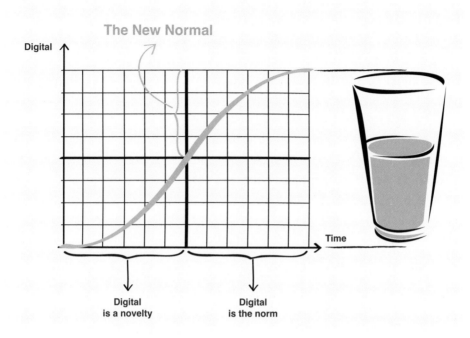

That S-curve of digital adoption occurred in about a decade. From 2010 till 2020, we saw the full impact of the S-curve play out in full force. My children were teenagers during that period and can hardly remember a time when 'digital' was not there. They are the internet generation that takes online connectivity, and digital for granted.

I am not blind to the negative elements related to digitalisation. Every innovation has its sharp edges and drawbacks. When you look at the addictive powers of digital technology, it is frightfully mind blowing. TikTok was not just one of the fastest growing apps of all times, it also appears to be one of the most addictive. The amount of time spent there is downright scary: up to 95 minutes per day per user, back in 2022.

Today this generation has Zero Tolerance for digital failure. Because anything 'normal' should just work. Like electricity. It was 'magic' 100 years ago. Today we expect to plug a vacuum cleaner into the socket in our wall and it should function flawlessly. The magic is gone. Only frustration remains when it does not work.

Greek American architect Nicholas Negroponte's book *Being Digital* was one of the most important influences on my professional career. He was the creative founding father of the MIT Media Lab, which he established to encourage different disciplines to cross-pollinate each other. And the result is truly fascinating: computer scientists collaborate with architects and artists with psychologists, all the while mingling with hard-core nerds.

In *Being Digital* he claimed there were only two types of companies: 'Bits' companies, like banks or insurance companies, that were in the business of information. And 'real' companies, that did not just shift information from here to there in a database, but that moved around 'atoms'. If you were a cement company, you were hauling atoms instead of bits. But in this amazing body of work, Negroponte predicted that eventually ALL Atoms companies would become Bits companies. Even the cement company would over time become dependent on digital processes, digital flows and digital interactions.

It has been an amazing privilege to watch Negroponte's predictions unfold over the course of my career. I have witnessed the transition from Atoms to Bits in virtually every market, every sector and every geography.

Magic became Normal.

NEW NORMALS AND THE GREAT ACCELERATION

Since the publication of *The Never Normal* I have been trying to figure out what the Next New Normal would be. I tried to observe the world of technology and innovation as closely as possible, to deduce what the Next New Thing would be and to fit that into a new definition of 'normal'. But I had to give up on that. There were just too many things that were materialising into normalcy, all at the same time. Instead of trying to chase the New Normal, I decided we would probably have many New NormalS.

NormalS with a Capital S at the end. Plural.

The pandemic was obviously a great accelerator of that transition. For many organisations, 2020 (and beyond) was a 'digital stress test' to see if they could survive in a world where digital was basically the only option.

Magic had become Normal just in time. Imagine if the pandemic had happened 20 years earlier, when we were still dialling into Internet Service Providers with modems, and when graphics would painstakingly slowly appear on our screens. The outcome would have been disastrous, right?

Post-pandemic, two interesting things crystallized. The first is that many companies realised that digital was way more than just the cherry on the cake. Before the pandemic, many of them had already developed their digital capabilities, but it was only *during* the pandemic that they realised how much more of their business could be done digitally. They saw how they could reach their customers via digital channels and operate their processes with digital means.

But secondly, and perhaps even more telling, was that many companies recognised that a significant part of their transformation efforts had merely been a matter of 'digital translation'. They had taken their old analogue processes and painted a little layer of 'digital veneer' on top, hoping it would hold up. Alas, those efforts proved below par. **Instead of digitising old analogue methods, it became clear that they had to completely rethink their processes for a world where digital had become normal.** Since digital translation does not really scale, true digital transformation is crucial.

THE S-CURVE AS A MECHANISM

I am a huge fan of Carlota Perez. In my opinion, she is one of the leading economic thinkers of our time. She has described the power of S-curves in detail in her work, and has proven that S-curves continuously materialise in economic history: the Industrial Revolution, the age of steam, the rise of railroads, the advent of mass production, etc. Repeatedly, we see the same S-curve patterns of innovation emerge.

These cycles used to take about 20 to 30 years to emerge and evolve from 'magic' to 'normal'. But today, this process is accelerating. The cycles of innovation are heating up, and whereas the 'digital' curve took a good 10 years, the next waves (like generative AI) could materialise in a fraction of that time. That means that instead of the one big wave of innovation that you had to catch in your professional career, you might now see three, or four waves. Your kids might see five, or seven. We seem to be heading towards more disruption, more quickly, with innovation cycles heating up and escalating with increased frequency.

Every time we see one of these S-curves move from magic to normal, we see potential for disruption. It is the classic Schumpeterian creative destruction, where some of the old guard just does not 'get it', and at the same time this produces enormous opportunities for new players to come in and eat someone's lunch. Creative destruction might therefore happen more frequently, offering more opportunities for entrepreneurial risk-takers, who want to ride the magic wave. Those who do will be challenged by the next S-curve that is just around the corner. Or not? The fundamental question is this: are things *really* heating up or is this just an illusion.

Frederik Anseel, Senior Deputy Dean at the UNSW Business School in Sydney, believes that we may be suffering from 'chronocentrism': the tendency of people and cultures to view their own time as the most important and to assume that the things they value are the most valuable. In other words, every generation throughout history tends to believe they live in unprecedented times, and that extraordinary events are changing the course of humanity.

Today, a popular term is 'polycrisis', coined and made famous by Adam Tooze, Director of the European Institute and nonresident scholar at Carnegie Europe and a professor of history at Columbia University. Tooze describes a polycrisis as, *'A series of shocks that, on the surface, appear independent of each other, but are interconnected and closely intertwined. The aggregation of those crises then becomes more than the sum of its parts.'*

These two beliefs are orthogonal. From a chronocentric perspective, we could view the current era as particularly significant and unique in human history, as it is marked by a high degree of global interconnectedness and a rapid pace of technological change. However, from a broader historical perspective, it can be argued that the world has faced many similar challenges in the past, and that the current moment is simply the latest iteration in a long line of human struggles.

SEISMIC SHOCKS

So, what is next? What can we expect from the next post-digital decade?

When I look to the future, I think there is but a very slim chance that the ride ahead will get any smoother. Instead, I think we may have to brace for quite a bumpy ride. A ride with even more Seismic Shocks. In Star Trek parlance we must activate our long-range sensors and pick up any distortions on our path. Those distortions are exploitable, rife with possibilities and form the very essence of opportunity.

TECHNOLOGICAL SHOCKS

The most obvious and logical next set of Seismic Shocks will undoubtably be technological in nature. The engineer in me gets excited when I think about the decade ahead. Today we are quite proud of our current post-pandemic digital New Normal. We are smug about our smartphones, apps, platforms and ubiquitous connectivity. The chances are very high that in 10 years we will look back at today, and find it quite rudimentary, possibly even naive and primitive.

To quote Douglas Adams again (I warned you that he is my favourite writer): *'Far out in the uncharted backwaters of the unfashionable end of the western spiral arm of the Galaxy lies a small unregarded yellow sun. Orbiting this at roughly ninety-two million miles is an utterly insignificant little blue green planet whose ape-descended life forms are so amazingly primitive that they still think digital watches are a neat idea.'*

When we look at the technological Seismic Shocks that lie ahead, a few major outlines emerge.

THE COGNITIVE ERA

The first is the evolution towards the Cognitive Era. The post-digital era will be one where intelligence seems to be embedded in every aspect of business and the economy. Not too long ago, the term 'Big Data', entered common parlance in reference to the then emerging 'Big Tech' players like Amazon and Meta that were amassing vast amounts of information, unheard of in the history of information technology. That is when companies like Google started to build new techniques to harness such gigantic amounts of data and information. But in the normalising second half of the S-curve, every company has essentially become a Big Data company.

The adage of processing information was simple: 'If you want to connect the dots, you have to collect the dots.' Many companies have spent considerable energy and effort to 'collect' the dots, but the challenge ahead is to see the patterns, to understand the complexities, to turn the Big Data into practical knowledge and then be able to act intelligently on that.

That's where the 'Cognitive Era' comes in. Artificial Intelligence has been around since the 1950s as a concept and has lived through many winters, but only now do we have the computing power and processing force to grasp its enormous potential. We were introduced to the concept of 'Generative AI' in 2022. First, with the generation of images via deep learning models like OpenAI's DALL-E 2, Stability AI's Stable Diffusion and Discord's Midjourney. Later, with the amazing chatbot capabilities of ChatGPT, also from OpenAI. Throughout this period, the mainstream audience started to understand just how powerful this set of generative tools could become in the 'Cognitive Era'.

But that is just one vector. Look at the amazing amount of funding going towards the metaverse, not in the least the billions of dollars spent by Meta, the parent company of Facebook, to develop the tools, technology and content for virtual worlds. The average reader of this book is perhaps not yet spending most of their time on an Oculus Quest, but our 19-year-old son is an avid VR-gamer, and for him this is already way beyond 'magic'. Virtual reality is normal for him.

After the enormous crypto and Web3 hype, we saw the almost total collapse of the entire industry. The FTX collapse became the Lehman Brothers moment of that sector, and it created a domino effect that rippled through the entire world of crypto. But the concepts, ideas and technologies that underpin the mechanism of Web3 are not dead. To the contrary. Over the coming years, we are bound to see enormous creative efforts from start-ups and entrepreneurs that will use the essential building blocks of Web3 to rebuild the entire web infrastructure in ways that offer more power to the consumers.

Generative AI, autonomous automation, Web3, the unleashing of the real power of Big Data, the capabilities of the metaverse, quantum computing, the list goes on and on. There will be no shortage of technological Seismic Shocks, fuelled by venture capital markets, and created by a myriad of hopeful, eager and hungry engineers and entrepreneurs wanting to build the next 'magic'.

BIOLOGICAL SHOCKS

As excited as I get about the Technological Seismic Shocks ahead, I must acknowledge that they are NOT going to be the only ones. And perhaps not even the most impactful ones either. The pandemic has shown us how countries, regions, societies, and even humankind can be completely disrupted by biological Seismic Shocks.

When the pandemic hit us, I rewatched Bill Gates' historical TED Talk from 2015, where he calmly outlined the next potential big global disaster: 'If anything kills over 10 million people in the next few decades, it's most likely to be a highly infectious virus rather than a war. Not missiles, but microbes.'

It is perplexing to watch this talk, recorded five years before a bat from Wuhan would completely change the world overnight. As Bill Gates pointed out back in 2015, this could perhaps have been avoided with a limited budget: *'I don't have an exact budget for what this would cost, but I'm quite sure it's very modest compared to the potential harm. The World Bank estimates that if we have a worldwide flu epidemic, global wealth will go down by over three trillion dollars and we'd have millions and millions of deaths. These investments offer significant benefits beyond just being ready for the epidemic.'*

Well. We should have listened better, that is for sure. Today, the COVID-19 period seems mostly behind us, now that even the last Zero-COVID believers are abandoning that concept. But when we look at the enormous impact of that Biological Seismic Shock, we should be careful to rule out that this could ever happen again.

ECOLOGICAL SHOCKS

Perhaps the most visible set of Seismic Shocks today are the ecological ones. It was the main concern before the pandemic, and it is by far the biggest one post-pandemic. In the US, the National Center for Environmental Information has started mapping all the weather and climate disasters since 1980, where the overall damages and costs reached or exceeded USD 1 billion. When I was writing this chapter in the early days of 2023, the database had no less than 341 events, where climate disasters caused more than USD 1 billion in damage. The total cost of these 341 events exceeded USD 2.475 trillion.

The environmental challenges facing the world today are vast. Global warming is causing changes in global temperature patterns and leading to more frequent and intense extreme weather events, rising sea levels, and melting polar ice caps. The impact is tangible on business, too. In the Summer of 2022, ongoing drought and low water levels of the Rhine threatened the supply security of the German industry, to give one 'small' example.

On top of that we have the incredible loss of biodiversity resulting from defor-estation, overfishing, and pollution, which is threatening the stability of entire ecosystems. The release of pollutants into the air and water, such as chemicals and plastic waste, is harming human and wildlife health, and causing long-term damage to the planet's natural systems.

With these pressures on our planet's resources, we are bound to endure increasing numbers of environmental Seismic Shocks that will have far-reaching and long-lasting impact on both the environment and human society. Everyone remembers the school strikes just before the pandemic, with Greta Thunberg leading a next generation revolution. But that was just the warm up act.

SOCIAL SHOCKS

Perhaps what worries me most in this list is the potential for a significant in-crease in Social Seismic Shocks. These can have a significant impact on so-ciety, causing widespread disruption, destabilisation, and changes in social norms, values, and behaviour.

Political upheavals and instability, combined with economic crises as we have seen post-pandemic, will only amplify the potential for social shocks. From the *gilets jaunes* in France, to the storming of the United States Capitol, or the equivalent in Brazil, we see the signs unfolding globally. These social shocks can lead to changes in the political, economic, and social systems, and can have far-reaching and long-lasting impact on individuals, communities, and entire societies.

GEOPOLITICAL SHOCKS

The tectonics of our geopolitical landscape are shifting in a major way as well. I remember growing up during the Cold War in a deeply divided Europe. The USSR and the USA were battling it out in a global display of innovation strength and technological pyrotechnics. From the space race to the nuclear rivalry, technology lay at the very heart of a long cold war that occasionally flared up in heated incidents, but luckily never ignited a full blown WWIII. Although it did come extremely close on several occasions.

When the Berlin Wall fell in 1989, many were convinced this would herald a new age of global understanding, and that the entire world would adopt a standard operating procedure, based on Western capitalism. That was a fundamental intellectual mistake. The world today has probably not been more fragile and politically uncertain since WWII. Despite the global mechanisms in place, ranging from the United Nations to the collections of G20, G8 and G7, we seem to have less stability, more uncertainty and a clear increase in geopolitical unrest.

The obvious example was the Russian invasion of Ukraine that suddenly burst onto the global scene at the onset of 2022. But this conflict is also the sorrowful result of fluctuating fault lines in the world economy. Like the tectonic plates that cover the earth and are constantly moving, forcing themselves with enormous power against each other and thus resulting in devastating earthquakes, the flux of geopolitical tectonics is creating massive fault lines.

Today we also have a new cold war on our hands, this time between the USA and the People's Republic of China. Since China joined the World Trade Organization in 2001, the economic rise of the PRC has been nothing short of spectacular. China emerged as an incredibly strong economic player, and a vital part in the globalised supply chain of virtually every market, from pharmaceuticals to electronics, consumer goods and machinery.

Fed by the spark of the Industrial Revolution, England became the foremost industrial nation in the nineteenth century. England became known as the 'workshop of the world', and English products, from locomotives to textiles were found on all continents. By the 20th century, the United States had replaced the UK as the predominant manufacturing power. Today, we have witnessed another such fundamental substitution.

But China is not too content to remain just the 'factory of the world'. Many of us have grown up with Apple products that were 'designed in Cupertino, made in China'. But the ambitions of the People's Republic of China no longer stop at being the next 'workshop of the world'. Since the rise of Xi Jinping, China aspires to become the leading global innovation power by 2050. China wants to be globally leading and at the forefront of frontier innovations, modern engineering technologies, and disruptive technologies.

The result of those shifting tectonic plates is a complete polarisation of the world of technology. The global tech stack has been split in two: a Western technology stack dominated by American (and often Silicon Valley) companies, and an Eastern technology stack, dominated by Chinese technology players. The geopolitical differences between China and the US – with extreme measures like the CHIPS and Science Act that is meant to 'lower costs, create jobs, strengthen supply chains, and counter China' – make this situation even more complex and volatile.

NEVER NORMAL

I do not want to depress any readers at this point. On the contrary, I fundamentally believe that virtually ALL these Seismic Shocks bear enormous opportunities. Every seismic shock holds the potential for a systemic shift for the better.

But we must be realistic, we are entering a world that I labelled the 'Never Normal' where tiny shifts can have huge consequences. One of my favourite examples is probably the Suez Canal debacle of 2021, when its water course was fully blocked for six whole days by the Ever Given container ship. Memes surfaced, people laughed, and others despaired, while comparatively tiny bulldozers tried to free the enormous ship that refused to budge. The irony of the ship owner's enormous EVERGREEN inscription was not lost. Yet such a seemingly negligible event – compared to everything else going on in the world at the time – hugely disrupted our global supply chain for weeks and months. Several media sources ran features on how the Suez Canal crisis could 'unleash worldwide toilet paper shortages' and you may remember that the looming threat of worldwide toilet paper shortage was absolutely *no* laughing matter at that time.

The Johari Window technique was designed by Joseph Luft and Harrington Ingham in 1955 to help people better understand their relationships with themselves and others.

	Known to self	Not known to self
Known to others	OPEN	BLIND SPOT
Not known to others	HIDDEN	UNKNOWN

But you will probably be more familiar with former United States Secretary of Defence Donald Rumsfeld's simplified interpretation of it when he introduced the concept of 'Unknown Unknowns' in a 2002 press conference. 'Unknown Unknowns' are situations where individuals or organisations are unaware of their lack of knowledge or understanding about a particular topic. In other words, they are not only ignorant about something but also unaware that they are ignorant about it.

Or as he put it: 'As we know, there are known knowns; there are things we know we know. We also know there are known unknowns; we know there are some things we do not know. But there are also unknown unknowns – the ones we don't know we don't know.'

The concept of the 'unknown unknowns' highlights that we always need to consider the potential of unforeseen events and outcomes in decision-making and planning. And that is crucial in the Never Normal.

GRADUALLY, THEN SUDDENLY

Let me explain with the concept of 'Gradually, then Suddenly'. The phrase is attributed to American author and *enfant terrible* Ernest Hemingway, who used this line in *The Sun Also Rises.* In this novel, a character named Mike – based on Hemingway's real life friend Patrick Guthrie – is asked how he went bankrupt, and he responds, 'Two ways. Gradually, then suddenly.'

This is the type of behaviour and roller-coaster ride we are bound to experience in the Never Normal. I call them 'Hemingway Patterns'. You should be able to pick up some of the early tremors and rumblings to respond to these Hemingway Patterns. You will need to learn to pick up signals faster than before, and then find ways to act on them. The American-Canadian sci-fi author William Gibson – credited with popularising the term 'cyberspace' – taught us that, 'The future is already here – it's just not evenly distributed.' He suggested that new developments can be emerging gradually in some areas while remaining hidden or unnoticed in others, until they suddenly become widely apparent.

During the last couple of years, it has been fashionable to throw the 'VUCA' acronym at these phenomena. VUCA is an abbreviation for Volatility, Uncertainty, Complexity, and Ambiguity. The term was first introduced by the United States Army War College in the 1990s to describe the increasingly complex and unpredictable nature of the global political and economic environment following the end of the Cold War.

In business and management contexts, VUCA is often used to describe a similarly complex and unpredictable environment, where the pace of change is rapid, and the future is difficult to predict. **Leaders and organisations that operate in a VUCA environment need to be agile and adaptable and able to make decisions quickly and effectively despite a high degree of uncertainty and ambiguity.**

VUCA became a framework for understanding and responding to the uncertainties and complexities of the situation, rather than as a set of specific strategies or solutions. That is exactly what I do not like about it. VUCA perfectly describes the concept of the Never Normal but does not offer a solution or a way forward, to perceive and manage the Hemingway Patterns.

The BANI framework was an attempt to fill this gap. It was developed by Jamais Cascio, a San Francisco-based author and futurist, who, among other things, worked for The Institute for the Future in Palo Alto. The BANI framework is an approach to help us understand and respond to a rapidly changing environment. Like VUCA, BANI is an acronym that stands for four different concepts: Brittle, Anxious, Non-Linear, and Incomprehensible. However, the two frameworks approach the problem from slightly different angles. While VUCA describes the environment as being volatile, uncertain, complex, and ambiguous, the BANI framework describes how organisations and individuals can respond to that environment.

For example, the concept of brittleness refers to the way that systems and organisations can become fragile and prone to failure in a rapidly changing environment. Anxiety refers to the way that people may become stressed and overwhelmed in the face of uncertainty and complexity. Non-linearity refers to the way that small changes can have disproportionate and unpredictable effects. While incomprehensibility refers to the way that it can be difficult to make sense of complex and rapidly changing situations.

Overall, the BANI framework can be seen as a way of understanding how people and organisations are likely to *react* to the challenges of a VUCA environment, while VUCA itself is a more general framework for understanding the nature of the environment itself.

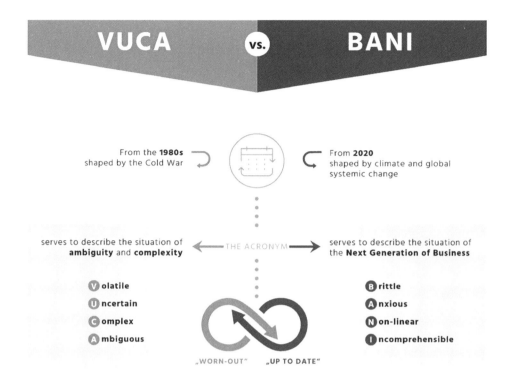

FOUR CHARACTERISTICS

To make the Never Normal more tangible, I have tried to look at it from four different dimensions and describe its four main 'characteristics':

1. SuperFluidity
2. NonLinearity
3. HyperConnectedness
4. UltraSpeed

SUPERFLUIDITY

SuperFluidity describes an environment of constant change and flux, of rapid transformation. A world that requires constant adaptation, and a business reality that is perpetually in motion.

As we should have shed our chronocentric bias by now, we realise that this is nothing new. The Greeks already described this liquid state about 2.500 years ago as *panta rhei*, which can be translated as everything flows or everything is in flux. The phrase is attributed to the ancient philosopher Heraclitus, who believed that the universe was in a constant state of change and opined that, 'You cannot step into the same river twice.'

The concept of *panta rhei* reflects a view of the world as being dynamic and constantly evolving, rather than static and unchanging. It suggests that change is an inherent part of the natural order and that everything is connected in a continuous process of transformation.

In the Never Normal, this concept is going into overdrive: from flux to Super-Fluidity.

SuperFluidity in business refers to the ability of organisations to rapidly adapt to change and swiftly respond to new opportunities and challenges. In today's quickly changing world, businesses are facing unprecedented levels of volatility, uncertainty and complexity, driven by factors such as technological innovation, globalisation, and shifting consumer preferences. As a result, companies need to be able to quickly pivot and adjust their strategies, processes and operations to keep pace with these changes.

SuperFluidity in business can manifest in several ways, including:

- **Agile decision-making**: The ability to quickly make decisions and take action, without being bogged down by bureaucracy and red tape.
- **Flexible operations**: The ability to quickly adjust operations and processes to meet changing customer demands and market conditions.
- **Rapid innovation**: The ability to quickly develop and bring new products and services to market, ahead of competitors.
- **Resilience**: The ability to quickly recover from setbacks and failures, and to bounce back stronger.

SuperFluidity has become a critical success factor for organisations. Those that can swiftly adapt and respond to change are better able to survive and thrive in an increasingly competitive and fast-paced business environment. However, achieving SuperFluidity can be challenging, as it requires the adoption of new ways of working, embracing new technologies, and continuously learning and evolving.

Stephen Hawking famously said, 'Intelligence is the ability to adapt to change.' In the Never Normal, we are going to need a lot of intelligence to adapt to SuperFluidity.

NONLINEARITY

The second characteristic of the Never Normal is that we will see a lot of nonlinear opportunities. Instead of looking straight down the traditional swimming lane in our familiar markets and traditional industries, we will need to be able to look OUTSIDE traditional boundaries.

Two examples to illustrate. The first is Amazon. I am old enough to remember when Amazon was an online website where you could buy a book or a CD. Then Amazon became the 'Everything Store'. In 2006, it also launched Amazon Web Services or AWS, providing on-demand cloud computing platforms and APIs to individuals, companies, and governments. This approach raised quite a few eyebrows: why would an online retailer like Amazon want to *share* its technology with potential competitors?

AWS was a completely novel concept that allowed businesses to rent computing resources and storage from Amazon's data centres, so that they could avoid the cost of building and maintaining their own IT infrastructures. This was a significant departure from Amazon's core business of selling books and other consumer goods online and it represented a bold and unconventional move for the company.

By launching AWS, Amazon was able to leverage its existing technology and infrastructure to create a new and innovative service that disrupted the traditional IT industry. This nonlinear approach to business allowed Amazon to tap into a new market, and to generate significant revenue from a source that had not previously been a part of its core business. And today, AWS has evolved to become one of the main engines of profit inside the Amazon universe.

A second example is what is happening in the automotive industry. We see companies like SONY teaming up with Honda to build an automobile. The idea that a consumer electronics expert has decided to get into the car business is a classic example of nonlinear thinking. At the same time Toyota is building their futuristic 'Woven City', where cars are merely an afterthought. Or we find Best Buy and ByteDance moving into healthcare, as are many others like Amazon. Netflix has been investing in mobile gaming. Media companies like the BBC have been offering training courses. The Never Normal completely redefines a company's relationship with an industry.

Unlike linear thinking, which relies on a step-by-step process of logical reasoning and analysis, this type of unconventional, extra-industry, nonlinear thinking is much more open, intuitive and creative. It involves making connections between seemingly unrelated ideas or concepts. It is about recognising that the solutions that worked in the past may not be relevant to the current situation.

HYPERCONNECTEDNESS

My second mainstream book was *The Network Always Wins*. The New Normal dynamic – where digital became normal – had an incredibly significant impact on business and the economy, but then I came to realise that the network effect was the interesting part of that equation.

To quote Joe MacMillan in the brilliant series *Halt and Catch Fire,* 'Computers aren't the thing. They're the thing that gets us to the thing.' Digital was not really the thing. I came to understand that, in a hyperconnected world, networks were the thing.

Hyperconnection is characterised by a complex web of relationships and interactions between people, devices, and systems, pushing an intricate, heavy and ultrafast flow of information. This continuous motion of data and ideas not only creates new opportunities for collaboration and innovation, but it also poses new challenges for privacy, security, crime, truth, polarisation and information management. It impacts everything that has to do with human relations: from our work and society to the market, the economy and politics.

Overall, a hyperconnected world represents a fundamental shift in the way people and organisations relate to one another. It requires new approaches, new processes, new structures and new strategies.

ULTRA-SPEED

The result is a world that seems to evolve faster than ever before. Gradually to suddenly, and all at the same time. Again, the pandemic was an excellent example of these Hemingway Patterns. Not only did the world come to a complete stop on the one hand, winners and losers emerged at great speed on the other.

One of my favourite expressions of the ultra-speed in pandemic times was how the market value of Zoom (which was merely an incremental innovation of previous tools like Skype or Webex) skyrocketed in an exponential manner. It was worth more on the stock exchange, at one point, than the combined value of seven of the largest airlines. A snapshot for sure, but also an excellent example of ultra-speed.

The impact of this ultra-speed on organisations is huge. Companies will need to adapt how they make decisions, how they solve problems and how they build strategies, if they do not want to be outpaced. Individuals will need to develop new skills if they want to stay relevant. Leadership and management must be rethought, with more agile methodologies or design thinking. Governance structures will have to adapt.

And at the same time, organisations will also need to maintain a careful balance between the benefits of this ultra-speed and a more thoughtful and reflective approach that keeps their organisations human and allows them to navigate risk in an intelligent manner.

THE CUCKOO CLOCK

I think I can almost hear you grumbling from behind this book, 'What does this Never Normal mean? How can these characteristics be seen as mechanisms or levers for change? How can this be a GOOD thing?

I never said it was easy.

It would be incredibly naive to think that in the post-pandemic world, we would just be able to go back to peace and quiet. Instead, I fundamentally believe that this Never Normal world will be characterised by nonlinear opportunities, superfluid agility, hyperconnected realities, and ultra-speed. That can be a good thing. It reminds me of a famous scene in the 1949 classic film, *The Third Man*. In that movie, a character called Harry Lime (played by Orson Welles) tells the protagonist Holly Martins (played by Joseph Cotten) a story about a cuckoo clock he purchased in Switzerland.

He says: *'In Italy, for 30 years under the Borgias, they had warfare, terror, murder and bloodshed, but they produced Michelangelo, Leonardo da Vinci and the Renaissance. But in Switzerland, they had brotherly love, they had five hundred years of democracy and peace – and what did that produce? The cuckoo clock.'* Similarly, in the world of business, the stress and volatility of the Never Normal could very well lead to breakthroughs or innovations that might not have been possible under more stable or predictable conditions. The pressure of competition, the need to respond to changing market conditions, and the demands of customers can all be powerful motivators for change and innovation.

And Ørsted – once one of the most fossil fuel intensive energy companies in Europe – is perhaps one of the most apt examples of this. Ørsted realised that its business model was coming to an end because of the growing urgency of the climate emergency and the political, social and commercial response to that. They decided to completely reinvent themselves into a global green renewable energy provider. Quite successfully, I might add. Today, most of their energy production comes from renewable sources, and it is a global leader in offshore wind. The company has been able to grow their business while reducing their carbon emissions by no less than 86%.

So, I fundamentally see two thoroughly different ways to respond to the Never Normal: robustness and resilience. Both concepts are related to the ability of systems to withstand and recover from disruptions, but they are very different in important ways.

Robustness, on the one hand, refers to the ability of a system to maintain its normal functioning in the face of disruption. A robust system is one that can resist or absorb shocks without being significantly affected or disrupted. In the context of engineering or technology, this might involve designing a product or system that can continue to operate even if certain components fail or malfunction. But in a business context, robustness means that you can operate, even if the going gets tough. Almost every business showed tremendous robustness during the pandemic.

Resilience, on the other hand, refers to the ability of a system to adapt to new conditions and recover quickly from disruptions or shocks like an economic crisis or a natural disaster. This might involve developing contingency plans, building redundancies into critical systems, or even cultivating a culture of preparedness and adaptability. So, resilience does not only mean you can bounce 'back', but it also means that you can absorb disruptive energy and use it to bounce 'forward'.

In other words, robustness focuses on the ability of a system to withstand disruptions without being significantly affected, while resilience focuses on the ability of a system to recover from disruptions and adapt to the new conditions, to thrive in the Never Normal. Robustness is about survival. Resilience is about thriving. It is status quo versus progress. Stability versus motion.

THRIVING IN THE NEVER NORMAL

So how does this translate? How can companies leverage the power of the Never Normal and thrive in this context? What does it mean for organisations, teams and individuals?

MINDSET

In my opinion, one of the consequences is that we will need more people with a 'Flux' mindset to harness the resilience required in the Never Normal. Those who have a mental state of agility and flexibility characterised by a willingness to embrace change, to let go of old habits and ways of thinking, and to continually learn and grow.

This flux mindset will be characterised by:

- ♥ **Adaptability**: The ability to respond to new situations and changing circumstances quickly and effectively.
- ♥ **Creativity**: The ability to generate new ideas and solutions, and to approach problems from different angles.
- ♥ **Resilience**: The ability to bounce back from setbacks and failures and to use these experiences as opportunities for learning and growth.
- ♥ **Open-mindedness**: The ability to consider new ideas and perspectives and to be willing to challenge one's own assumptions and beliefs.
- ♥ **Curiosity**: The desire to explore new ideas, concepts, and experiences and to approach the world with a sense of wonder and curiosity.

Overall, the flux mindset is a mindset of constant adaptation and growth fit for a rapidly changing world. One that embraces the uncertainty and ambiguity of the modern world. One that sees change as an opportunity for learning and development. One that is open to the magic of a *panta rhei* environment.

SKILLS

A big element in this will be the skills spectrum. Companies used to focus on sourcing employees with 'narrow-band' skill sets, fit for the next task that lay dead-ahead and who stayed in their designated linear swimming lane. Companies eager to seek out nonlinear opportunities in this rapidly changing and unpredictable environment will need employees with 'broad band' skill sets; people capable of looking outside their swimming lane and seeing adjacent opportunities.

At the same time, the shelf life of skills is dropping at an alarming rate. I had the opportunity to become a research fellow at the MIT Sloan School of Management back in 2016. If you are not familiar with it, that is the business school of MIT, which trains some of the smartest kids in the world in the field of science and engineering. Some of its computer science professors openly told me that the rate of change in today's technological world creates huge issues in their curriculum. *'What we teach first year computer science students about AI for example, used to be outdated by the time they would graduate. Now, the rate of change is so high, that what we teach is outdated before they take their year-end exams.'*

In the super-speed environment of the Never Normal, companies will really need to develop a culture of continuous learning – of reskilling and upskilling – that encourages employees to keep developing new skills and knowledge. This means offering incentives for learning and development and creating a supportive environment that values learning and growth.

BEYOND DIGITAL

When I mentioned the difference between digital transformation and digital translation earlier, I remarked that companies need to fundamentally rethink their processes for a world where digital is normal. In the Never Normal we have to move beyond that.

Digital should not be an endpoint. Digital is merely one step in the direction of the Never Normal. We should be able to reimagine our way of working, our structures and processes to achieve the maximum flexibility and adaptability. I am not sure we will be able to do that with our current organisational design patterns.

Max Weber was a German sociologist, historian, jurist and political economist who is widely regarded as one of the founding fathers of modern sociology. But he is perhaps best known for his analysis of the role of bureaucracy in modern society. He believed that bureaucracy emerged naturally in response to the growth of modern industrial societies. Their scale required new forms of organisational structures to coordinate their large-scale activities. For Weber, bureaucracy was THE most efficient format for achieving this coordination because it relies on a system of rules and procedures that ensure rational, consistent and predictable behaviour.

Bureaucracy may have been the ideal organisational design pattern for the Industrial Revolution. But in the Never Normal, we will have to make a quantum leap in organisational design. **As I wrote earlier in this chapter, we must go beyond 'digital'. We will have to adopt a more organic way of working, and create much more flexible and collaborative environments that encourage creativity, innovation, and employee empowerment.** We will need to foster open and inclusive cultures that value diversity of opinions and encourage feedback. We will need to provide psychological safety and opportunities for employees to experiment and try new things and encourage them to come up with new ideas and think outside the box.

End results will and should become much more important than controlling the fixed processes that lead to the result. You will need to allow your employees the flexibility to find the best way to deliver these results, by creating a sense of purpose and helping them understand how their work contributes to the company's overall goals.

It is important to note that there *is* a time and place for bureaucracy in some organisations, especially those that need to operate with strict regulations or adhere to rigid standards of quality control. Most organisations, especially the large ones, will need to adhere to a bimodal way of performing: procedures where safety and status quo are important and agility for Never Normal situations. But it is safe to say that organisations will not survive with bureaucracy alone. They will need a more organic operating system.

GREAT EXPECTATIONS

I want to end this chapter with some musings about expectations. As Alexander Pope once said: **'Blessed is he who expects nothing, for he shall never be disappointed.'** Over the years I have been prone to 'over-excitement'. It is probably one of my best and worst characteristics at the same time. When I see a new piece of technology, often in its infancy, I become absolutely thrilled. I cannot wait to see it mature, become mainstream and then use it. You could probably blame that tendency on the 'Nerd-DNA' that is so typical of us engineers.

But I have also been disappointed quite a bit.

Take autonomous cars. They were perhaps one of the biggest duds of the New Normal. And that had everything to do with how we all overhyped their capabilities. I had the chance to sit in a Google car more than six years ago. That was brilliant. But when I recently bought a brand-new car, it was far from self-driving. Even Tesla, which pioneered some of the narrative, is now facing criminal charges since their claims to self-driving were basically 'smoke and mirrors'.

At the end of 2022, Ford and Volkswagen, two of the world's largest automakers, shut down Argo AI, their joint effort to develop self-driving cars. They had poured billions of dollars into that start-up, which was comprised of more than 1000 engineers, but the results just did not materialise. When they pulled the plug, the CEO of Ford, Jim Farley stated: 'Profitable, fully autonomous vehicles at scale are a long way off and we won't necessarily have to create that technology ourselves. 'At the same time, General Motors' self-driving start-up, Cruise, is continuing their quest, but it lost USD 1.4 billion in 2022.

So, who is right? Ford and Volkswagen to call it quits, or GM to continue (together with funding from Microsoft) to keep working on self-driving cars? Whatever the case, it's probably safe to say that autonomous driving is experiencing some winter of sorts. With autonomous delivery vehicle maker Nuro laying off about 20% of its workforce end of 2022 and Waymo announcing layoffs in January 2023, with rumours that it would kill its trucking program.

This is probably the most helpful and clear graph I have ever observed about the reality of our emotional journey in technology. The blue S-curve illustrates how innovation tends to develop and the dotted red line represents our human expectations.

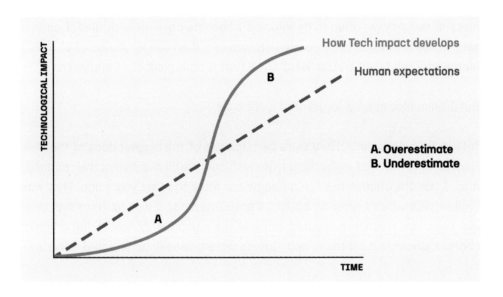

It clearly exposes two fundamentally different dynamics. In the beginning, our expectations FAR surpass the reality of how innovation unfolds, which clearly leads to frustration and disappointment. On the other hand, as technology matures, we tend to UNDERestimate its real impact in the long term. That is when it surpasses our expectations. By far. That is close to magic, in my opinion.

CONCLUSION

Winston Churchill's famous quote *'If you don't take opportunity by the hand, it will take you by the throat'* is a powerful reminder of the importance of being proactive and seizing opportunities to control one's own destiny. In today's Never Normal world this quote takes on even greater significance. The pace of change is faster than ever, and companies that fail to adapt risk being left behind or even becoming irrelevant.

But there is good news; great even. With change comes opportunity, and those that can identify and capitalise on emerging trends can gain a significant competitive advantage. It is physics, really. You use the energy that could otherwise break you, to propel yourself forward. Instead of fighting against the wind and almost blowing away, you turn around and build sails. And re-invent yourself like a phoenix.

CHAPTER 9

THE NEVER NORMAL CUSTOMER

'IT IS NO LONGER THE BEST TEAM THAT WINS, BUT RATHER **THE TEAM THAT ADAPTS BEST** TO NEW CIRCUMSTANCES'

MARC LAMMERS, DUTCH FIELD HOCKEY COACH, OLYMPIC GOLD AND
SILVER MEDALLIST

ONE BLACK SWAN AFTER ANOTHER

John Lewis, the CEO of the United Nations Federal Credit Union, gave a presentation recently at a conference in Memphis. I was in the audience. After his talk, I asked him, 'John, what is your biggest concern right now?' I will never forget his answer, 'My biggest concern is currently changing every 12 hours.' I immediately understood him. When you think about all that has come our way in the past 24 months, it is almost unbelievable. You recognise the Never Normal that Peter Hinssen wrote about in Chapter 8 almost daily. The COVID crisis, logistical problems, price hikes, energy crisis, war in Ukraine, inflation, pressure on purchasing power… every month a new challenge has landed on the plates of many managers. The moment you think that things will calm down for a while, another bank (Silicon Valley Bank) collapses. It seems never-ending.

Nassim Nicholas Taleb released his book *The Black Swan* in 2007. It was an instant bestseller. **The essence of his book is very simple: we must watch out for that one unexpected moment that can turn an industry completely upside down.** Either you do not see a black swan heading towards you or you underestimate its impact. In both cases, it is likely that your company will react too late. I met Nassim at the Oslo Business Forum, in 2021, where we were both speakers. He said, 'The idea of one black swan is over. For the last few years, it has been one black swan after another.'

In fact, we have been moving from one crisis to the next for the past two decades. In 2001, there was 9/11 and a wave of terrorist attacks followed, in 2008, the financial crisis and, in addition, there is the climate crisis, perhaps the biggest chronic challenge that we face.

THE NEVER NORMAL CUSTOMER

Peter argues very convincingly in Chapter 8 that the world will never be stable again and he gives clear guidelines on how to deal with this. Customer behaviour has changed many times in response to the Never Normal world. Who would have ever thought that many people's showers would involve turning off the water while lathering up? You must have had an energy debate at your own kitchen table, right? Who could have predicted the rapid rise of home-delivered food in the pre-COVID era? The succession of shocks experienced by societies worldwide has led to new patterns and new ways of decision-making by customers. It is important to understand this evolution in thinking to properly serve the Never Normal customer, who:

1. Holds increasingly extreme opinions. Nuance is increasingly less common in public debates.
2. Is very concerned about society. The climate is now a topic of conversation in every family. Concerns are growing for a myriad of other worries beyond the climate such as inequality, poverty, education, etc.
3. Is open to new technology. Over the past two decades, technologies like the internet and the smartphone have drastically changed the way we 'customerise'. An openness to the rapid adoption of valuable tech has emerged.
4. Is losing interest in traditional jobs. Most companies face the difficulty of finding enough and the right people to maintain their customer experience. Fewer and fewer young people fancy a 'traditional' career. Scarcity in the labour market is an ongoing challenge.
5. Wants low exit barriers. Customer loyalty has declined. One of the reasons is the ease with which customers can change deliverers these days.

This chapter explores these characteristics of the Never Normal customer and offers proposals on how companies can address their needs.

1. INCREASINGLY EXTREME OPINIONS

One of the biggest challenges of our digital age is knowing what information to believe or not to believe. I am sometimes doubtful about the veracity of online information. Do you recognise this feeling? You may read something on the internet and spread the word only to find that it was fake news. Embarrassing! A photo of Lionel Messi proudly raising the football World Cup in the air became the most liked photo in the history of Instagram. At the time of writing, this photo has been liked more than 74 million times. Incredible! (Literally, it turns out.) Two weeks after its publication, it emerged that the cup Messi was holding was a replica, not the genuine World Cup, but the world did not even question it. We were all wrong!

The story of Messi's world cup is quite innocent. But fake news can lead to great tragedies. On Sunday, 4 December 2016, a man with a gun walked into a pizza restaurant. He began shooting to break the lock on a storage room door, and fortunately and miraculously, he did not hit anyone. Prior to this event, a series of fake news tweets had named the restaurant, Comet Ping Pong, as the headquarters for a paedophile community that purportedly included Hillary Clinton. It was rumoured that the FBI would investigate the case after finding suspicious information in Hillary's private emails. This prompted a lot of online chatter about #pizzagate and prompted a wave of threats against the owner of the pizza restaurant, culminating in the December shooting incident.

The power of fake news on a broad societal level was demonstrated on 6 January 2021 when Trump supporters stormed the Capitol in Washington, DC. Fake news creates instability and unrest in the population and at worst can be a threat to democracy.

Studies have shown that fake news spreads faster than real news.[69] Even if automated social media bots are filtered out of the study,[70] people tend to believe fake news if it fits into their existing thought patterns (logical). Even if the fake news does not fit into existing thought patterns, people are more likely to start believing it if they see that fake news often. This is the 'Illusory Truth Effect': the tendency to regard false information as correct after repeated exposure. This phenomenon was first identified in 1977 by at Villanova University and Temple University in the US. When first exposed to news, our brain compares that news with our existing knowledge. That initial benchmark determines initial credibility. The greater the repetition of a message, the more likely people are to spontaneously begin to believe it and the strength of their own existing knowledge diminishes.[71]

A study published in *Nature* magazine in October 2022 was the first to reveal the impact of the mass spread of fake news on the polarisation of ideas. Their research resulted in the Social Opinion Amplification Model (SOAM). Their model proves that extreme polarisation can effectively arise from the rapid spread of fake news through social media.[72] There are two ways to counter extreme polarisation. The first strategy is to ensure that messages cannot be shared more than five times by the same individual. This is difficult to do anything about. Only the social media companies themselves have an impact on this. The second strategy is to consistently share balanced opinions to the total population. This is where the traditional media, as well as companies, can play a significant role in lowering polarisation.

Everyone senses that there has been an increase in polarised discussions in recent years. In politics, as well as on social media and at some family tables, discussions are becoming more heated. Just think of the number of families that argued over COVID vaccines. Opinions in society used to be normally distributed like a classic Gaussian curve. Today, this curve seems to have been inverted with the ends of the curve containing many more people than the middle. While the majority used to have nuanced views on a lot of issues, today the tendency is towards having extreme views.

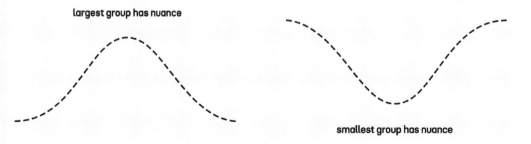

old world

largest group has nuance

new world

smallest group has nuance

2. MAJOR CONCERNS ABOUT SOCIETY

A lot has landed on our plates between 2020 and 2023: a global pandemic, a new large-scale war in Europe, an energy crisis, high inflation and obvious signs that the climate is heading in the wrong direction. Numerous heat waves, days when heat and cold records are broken, and the number of storms and floods are ever increasing.

This succession of societal shocks has created a higher level of awareness about global challenges amongst average consumers. *The Wall Street Journal* published a study conducted jointly with Deloitte showing that 40% of the population (across six countries) wants to be more actively involved in addressing social challenges. Many of them changed their buying routines and encouraged others to do the same.[73] **According to the researchers, we are entering 'an age of activism'**, a time when words are no longer enough and everyone in society – government, businesses, citizens – must join forces to tackle social problems.

The study also showed that during the last 12 months 38% of the population had taken affirmative action such as signing a petition, attending an event, or donating money to a campaign. Of all the challenges, climate topped the list of concerns; 64% of respondents put recycling and reuse at the top of their action list, followed by reducing single-use plastic and improving air quality. Incidentally, these results are identical across the six countries included in the survey. Climate concerns are increasingly becoming a universal theme. The extreme weather patterns of recent years are the main reason for this global concern.

Naturally, companies realise that the market's attitude in this area is changing at lightning speed. By identifying and responding to the public's concerns, companies can strengthen their reputations. Deloitte's study shows a correlation between being actively involved in social challenges and brand loyalty and sales. The younger the customer is, the stronger the correlation. Consumers between 18 and 25 years old are three times more likely to switch brands because of a lack of activism on the part of the producer than consumers aged 65 or older.

Fifty-eight percent of the market expects companies to adapt their ways of working to the new challenges in the world, 55% expect brands to co-build awareness around social issues and 41% expect companies to donate money to good causes. Consumers expect action, not just words. Action has the biggest impact on loyalty and brand perception.

One consumer concern is rising poverty and inequality in the world. Considering these concerns, Amazon decided to create a dedicated hub that features its most affordable products.[74] This hub also displays all major promotions and discounts for the most essential products. There is also the option to become a member of Prime Access. Prime is the subscription formula where customers get extra discounts, access to Prime Video (Amazon's Netflix) and faster deliveries. For 'regular' consumers, a membership costs USD 14.99 a month. More than 2 in 3 US households are members of Amazon Prime. Prime Access offers the same benefits at a discounted price of USD 6.99 a month. The cheaper membership is available to people who the government can confirm are less well-off. This example illustrates how companies can respond to social challenges through concrete actions. It is these kinds of initiatives that consumers expect from companies.

3. OPENNESS TO NEW TECHNOLOGY

Everyone has seen the graph, haven't they? The one that compares the adoption rates of newspapers versus radio versus TV versus the internet versus smartphones versus social media, visualised side by side. You know the conclusion: the adoption of each new medium happens faster and faster and faster.

Meanwhile, the increasingly rapid uptake of popular technology remains a given in our world. Compare, for example, the adoption rate of Facebook versus TikTok. Facebook was launched in 2004 and had a rather slow start in its first few years. By the end of 2006, the platform had 12 million users. By the end of 2012, eight years after its launch, Facebook had 1 billion users. By comparison, TikTok started up in 2016 (then called Douyin in China) and immediately saw rapid growth. By the end of 2018, two years after it started, TikTok already had 1 billion users. Things are moving faster and faster.

New technology trends usually start first with young people and are then very quickly followed by older generations. In any case, I discover many new apps from my children.

One of the technologies of the moment is the metaverse. Ever since Mark Zuckerberg changed the name of his company from Facebook to Meta in October 2021, the hype erupted. Since then, more money than ever has been flowing into virtual worlds and brands have become increasingly interested in them. However, three-dimensional virtual worlds, Mark Zuckerberg's dream, are not yet succeeding in winning over the masses. By early 2023, there will be between 60 and 90 million active VR headset users.[75] This is very low uptake relative to the investments in this technology. Does this suggest that the increasingly rapid uptake of new technology will come to an end after all?

The reason for the slow adoption of virtual worlds? Their user experience is considered substandard, and the content only appeals to a niche audience (mostly gamers). By the time this book will be published, Apple will have launched VR/AR glasses. Given Apple's reputation, it could well be that we will then suddenly find ourselves with a completely different interface. A better interface, coupled with their network of software developers, could boost adoption in the coming years. Consumers are open to new technology, but it is important that it can deliver the three benefits described in Chapter 7: efficiency, personalisation and creativity. TikTok's score is excellent for all three of these, while the metaverse has some progress to make on all three. Therein lies the explanation for the lower adoption.

Companies need to know which technology will best serve their relationship with the Never Normal customer. It is advisable to start working with new technologies yourself. If you want to experience the metaverse at a high level, visit a branch of Dreamscape or The Park Playground. These companies deliver an excellent experience and show you all their potential. Experiment yourself with all the AI applications you hear about. Even if only for 10 minutes, it will give you an idea about the possibilities. Then ask yourself the question, how can this technology provide value to my market and go from there. Once you can deliver that value, then the Never Normal customer is very quick to adopt new technology.

4. DECLINING INTEREST IN 'TRADITIONAL' JOBS

Attracting the right people to deliver an outstanding customer experience to customers has always been a challenge, but in these post-pandemic times, it has become even more difficult. The percentage of people voluntarily leaving their jobs is 25% higher than in the pre-COVID era.[76] A McKinsey study concluded that 40% of all employees in the US are considering changing jobs in the next three to six months.[77] In other words, four in 10 of your employees are considering changing jobs soon! Chances are, you yourself are currently in doubt about the future of your career.

Moreover, half of the working population has a 'quiet quitting' attitude: these employees come to work, but do not want to do anything more than what is strictly necessary.[78] Even in China, resistance to their notorious '996' system (working 9am to 9pm six days each week) is emerging. The Chinese are convinced that they can beat the Western world by working harder: more hours with more people. Recently, younger Chinese and even the Chinese middle class have been rebelling against this principle. There is talk of the 'lying flat movement' questioning the mentality of working more and more to support the economy.

Keeping, motivating and attracting talent is harder. Digital entrepreneur Gary Vaynerchuk talks about the 'never apply in the first place' generation. Many young people have no interest in working for a more 'traditional' company. They have no desire to climb up a traditional career ladder. Moreover, many of them also have less confidence in large companies that have a focus mainly on short-term share price. Many young people have seen their parents fired because of that share price. Too often, people who do their jobs well are asked to leave because of that short-term pressure on finances. Naturally, many young people will then think twice before joining a company with the same mindset. Young people today have more options to earn a living, so they can also consciously choose something else.

Tibeau Denamur is a young 25-year-old Flemish entertainer whose early success is an example of the various digital options that young people have today. You may not recognise his name, but he is the third most-listened-to Flemish artist on Spotify.[79] He has yet to beat top DJs Like Mike and Dimitri Vegas. His music is streamed an average of 2 million times a month. He makes Lofi Hip Hop, which is quiet background music that people put on to study or to lull hemselves to sleep. His 2 million streams earn him several thousand Euros a month. His passion allows him to make a good living. Tibeau works with music, but others excel at making videos, some are funny and build a community of followers on TikTok, some young people are good at trading crypto currencies. As their options increase, the need to choose a more traditional job decreases. This attitude combined with the retirement of baby boomers will only make the labour market tighten and this, in turn, puts a strain on the customer experience of many organisations.

5. THE NEVER NORMAL CUSTOMER LIKES LOW EXIT BARRIERS

Have you watched *Ted Lasso*? Or *Wednesday*? And what did you think of *Jack Ryan*? I really liked the new *National Treasure*; did you?

Have you seen one or more of these series? Then you are (in chronological order) a customer of Apple TV, Netflix, Amazon Prime Video and/or Disney Plus. Each of the streaming channels has its own top series running in mid-2023. They each invest billions a year to wow consumers with exceptional content. The more people talk about it or share their enthusiasm on social media, the more people want to watch. Are there many people who are customers of all four of these streaming services? Not in Europe, where an average family has two streaming subscriptions. In the United States, an average family effectively has four such subscriptions.[80] The adoption of these video on demand services saw tremendous growth during the COVID period.

However, *The Wall Street Journal* has found that a major loyalty problem has emerged in this market.[81] More and more families are becoming customers of, say, Netflix to watch its latest hit *Wednesday*, but immediately afterwards cancel their subscription. The trend is to subscribe only as long as needed to view a title. Nineteen percent of customers of companies like Netflix, AppleTV and Disney+ have taken out then discontinued three or more subscriptions in the past two years. An analysis of Netflix customer numbers illustrates the problem: almost half (45%) of those who subscribed in January 2022 cancelled their subscriptions within six months compared to 29% in 2020. In other words, acquisition costs are rising massively. They push people in at the front of the bus while others are falling out at the back. **The streaming market is characterised by very low exit barriers through which consumers try to maximise their economic value.**

In recent years, exit barriers – the cost for a customer to leave a supplier – have fallen in most industries. The main drivers are:
- ◆ *Increased competition*. Netflix's loyalty rates were higher a few years ago because there was no alternative. Now this market is highly competitive, and the players are formidable. This gives customers more options and customer loyalty drops.
- ◆ *More and better information*. Thanks to the internet and social media, customers are better informed than before. A well-informed customer can make better and more rational decisions and is more likely to switch to a better value alternative.

- *Digital convenience.* In the past, customers often had to go through a tedious procedure to change suppliers; today it can often be done with one (or even no) push of a button. If you want to switch from Uber to Lyft, you don't need anything. Both are side-by-side on your phone, so you only need to move your thumb a little more to the left or right.
- *Customer changes in perceptions and beliefs*: customers are evolving with the world and will look more for companies that fit their personal values, so a switch of supplier is happening faster than before.

There are few industries that are not affected. It is easy to switch telecom providers. You can keep your number and before you know it, you are with a different provider. Online shopping and e-commerce has made it simple for consumers to compare prices and promotions. This ease of use also increases their freedom to quickly switch to a different brand if they become dissatisfied with a company's service.

The offerings of pure digital banks like Revolut are a response to all the frictions customers have with traditional banks, making Revolut's interface very enticing. Whereas with a traditional bank it is not always easy to apply for a new credit card, for example, banks like Revolut have made this process almost automatic. With low barriers to entry and exit, a disgruntled customer can switch easily to a bank like Revolut.

Ultimately, low exit barriers are a good thing for us as customers. High competition, high transparency and a high risk of the customer switching to the competitor creates positive pressure on the customer experience. The only way to keep your customers on board is to offer them a good service and experience. However, this is not simple to accomplish in all sectors. In the world of content streaming, for example, people are still mainly hung up on the product. Disney, Netflix and Amazon are trying to poach each other's customers through cool content. In the end, they each have top series and the interface and price is about the same. Increased creativity is needed to keep the customer experience unique. Disney, Apple and Amazon have an advantage over other streaming services because the customer can access other services they offer, making the overall package more valuable to the customers. Netflix does not currently offer additional services. This has prompted Netflix to take refuge in an advertising model. This allowed them to lower the subscription prices. This new cheaper model had an immediate positive impact on the numbers of new subscriptions. Netflix gained 7.8 million new customers by the fourth quarter 2022 compared to a market prediction of 4.5 million.[82] This cheaper entry-level formula with an ad-based business model clearly helped to attract a wider audience but offered no improvement in the customer experience. I wonder when they will rethink their business model to offer the customer something more than only access to the next cool series. That is Netflix's challenge to put an end to high rates of subscriber turnover.

HOW TO ADDRESS THE NEEDS OF THE NEVER NORMAL CUSTOMER?

The world has been in a state of permanent turbulence for several years. This has had an impact on our customers. The major shocks in our society combined with the characteristics of the Never Normal customer create new opportunities. Changes in consumer behaviour have often been the driver towards the development of successful new businesses. Ultimately, a threat is usually an opportunity that you have not responded to or have been too slow to respond to. Viewed from this perspective we are entering an era of opportunity. Think back to the rise of Uber. The company was the first to address the frustration felt by many taxi customers by exploiting several existing technologies. Many new financial services emerged in the wake of the 2008 financial crisis. The chocolate brand Nutella was born out of a crisis. There was a global scarcity of chocolate at the end of World War 2. Ferrero, based at that time in the Piedmont region of northern Italy, turned this problem into an opportunity. They used hazelnuts, sugar and a little chocolate to create a chocolate paste they named Nutella. Changes in the market always create opportunities. You just need to spot them and take action.

I felt it was important to end this book with an overview of the main evolutions in consumer attitudes. This is the world in which we must make our diamonds shine permanently. In the first two parts of the book, important advice on how to deal with the Never Normal customer was already covered.

1. Increasingly extreme opinions: in a polarised world, it is important to ensure a positive mindset and approach. This is how you make a positive difference to your customers. This confirms the importance of the Top Gun Effect. In addition, leadership and communication from the leadership team will be extremely decisive here (both internally and externally). Chapter 4 'Believe!' covered this in detail.

2. Great concern for society: this confirms the importance of our social contributions to customer strategy. Increasing your circle of influence is the way to deal with this.

3. Openness to new technology: in Chapter 7 'When Digital Becomes Human', it became clear that technology is necessary to make the diamond shine, but it will have to be done mainly in combination with strong human attributes.

4. Declining interest in 'traditional' jobs. Your reputation and leadership style make a big difference in getting the right people on board. This is linked to the content from Chapter 4 'Believe!'

5. They like low exit barriers. Customer loyalty no longer starts with customers, but with companies. Do not ask the question: 'How can I make the customer more loyal to my company?'. Ask the question: 'How can my company show my loyalty to the customer?' The strategy from the 'Customer Loyalty Flywheel Effect' chapter will help you do this. Also, the philosophy around 'Effective Empathy' contributes to that brilliant diamond that makes people want nothing more than to be customers of your company.

If you manage to use the different components of the polished diamond and embrace them as a philosophy in your business, you have everything you need to give this Never Normal customer a fantastic customer experience.

EPILOGUE:
THE 100+ CONCRETE TIPS!

The subtitle of my book contains a rock-solid promise: 'with over 100 concrete tips to build a strong customer culture'. At the end of each chapter in the first two volumes, you already found a bunch of concrete tips to get started. If you counted carefully, you saw that the sum of all those tips per chapter does not yet equal 100.

To fulfil my promise to you, I have put together all the concrete tips from the chapters plus a whole series of tips that cannot be linked to a specific chapter. So here you have a nice overview with more than 100 customer experience tips to find concrete inspiration that will strengthen your own customer culture.

If you want to get started concretely with these tips, I recommend you buy (hard copy) or download (download is free) my 'How to Become a Shiny Diamond Workbook'. Then you can also start working with it in your daily practice.

You can download the workbook or buy a hard copy here.

Here we go!

1. If something goes wrong in your planning, proactively communicate the situation to the customer. Don't let the customer figure it out for themselves but be the first to suggest an alternative solution or timing.
2. If you have a client project that involves several parties, involve these parties from the beginning. Also introduce them to the customer in such a way that everyone is on the same team to help the customer properly.
3. Build long-term partnerships with suppliers. Make sure your suppliers become partners who enjoy working for you; this will benefit quality and continuity.
4. Rules and procedures are there to be broken 5% of the time. You have your processes, and you have your sense of touch. Allow your sense of touch to occasionally break the rules for the benefit of the customer.
5. If you want to give a presentation on customer-centricity to your employees, allow a satisfied as well as a dissatisfied customer to speak. But don't forget to frame this in a way that benefits your culture. The dissatisfied customer is not a reproach, but an opportunity to learn and become better.
6. Ask each employee if they have one idea to help customers better. Then give them the responsibility to implement their own idea. The leader's job is to make them succeed in that project.
7. In tough economic times, it is important to look for cheap ways to be even more customer-centric. If you then cut back on your CX, it will be difficult to bring it back up to par afterwards. Just when everyone else is doing less well, it is an opportunity to do better yourself.
8. Don't put all your resources into constantly coming up with new products; put enough resources into coming up with a better experience. Use part of your product budget for your customer experience.
9. When you communicate externally, always make it a positive message. Even if it is bad news, make sure there is a positive story attached to it.
10. Never talk about your own problems to your customers. They have 0% interest in that. But think about their problems and how you can solve them.
11. The media is often looking for negative stories about people and companies with problems; don't be tempted to join in that. Look at those negative stories as opportunities to do better yourself.

12. Compliment your customers. Highlight the good things you see from your customers.
13. Send customers a spontaneous gift when something nice has happened in their lives.
14. Send some handwritten cards to customers every week to congratulate or thank them.
15. Send a personal note along with your invoice, so it doesn't become so impersonal. Even make invoices fun.
16. Respond to your customers' social media posts: congratulate them, wish them well....
17. Radiate optimism, positivity and energy. You are looking forward to today!
18. Devise a 'pay it forward' philosophy that suits your business. What can your clients donate to people in need where you are the facilitator?
19. Look for what your company can do on a social level that also fits the sector you operate in. (e.g., Can an insurance broker in his municipality help make the municipality more bicycle safe?)
20. Identify the social issues that suit your company and formulate a positive opinion about them for yourself. Where relevant, you can then share that opinion. Not to seek polarisation, but to contribute positively.
21. Make a list of all the sustainability efforts your company is making and see how you can communicate that or decide which actions are still missing.
22. If you support charities, find a focus in that so you can also make it a story. A simple story that fits well with your company is the best one to tell.
23. Look at the list of SDGs and ask yourself: which one suits us best and can we also do our bit? Then you can take the appropriate action.
24. If there is ever negative news about your company, choose transparency in your communication.
25. Have your own way of communicating analysed. Where do you motivate or demotivate employees to be customer oriented? Learn to understand your own communication better in order to be a better leader.
26. Practise saying certain motivational phrases when employees have done something special for a customer, even if it took a bit more time and money from them. While doing so, restrain yourself from correcting them.

27. If you organise a brainstorm or workshop on CX, make it only about CX. Don't include anything else, and certainly not financial information, which indirectly sends the message that you always put efficiency and self-interest above the customer. Focus!

28. Dare to choose for the customer when there is an opposing interest and communicate this to your team. 'We accept short-term pain in order to win trust in the long term'.

29. Don't make customers pay for something that gives them no value.

30. If a mistake happened or there is a problem: solve it. Only then can you look at what really went wrong.

31. Believe in the 95%-5% rule and make decisions for the 95% of 'normal' customers who are not abusing loopholes in your system. Don't let the 5% ruin the experience of the 95% others.

32. Trust your team. Give them the tools to make customers happy and give them the freedom to choose what is best. Besides, they are often closer to the customer than you and may know better what works and what doesn't.

33. Inspire your team with 'random acts of kindness' that you set up for customers yourself. Invite them to do the same.

34. If something has gone wrong between an employee and a customer, the leader's job is to help the customer and support the employee.

35. Every week, share any positive messages you have received from a customer.

36. Work with a customer's 'quote of the week'.

37. If someone has done something exceptional to help a customer, put that employee in the spotlight (literally).

38. Look for small frictions in your customer relationship every month and resolve them every month. Involve employees in this process.

39. Organise a 'customer challenge' with your team every month. 'What are we going to do this month to make customers extra happy?'

40. Start every meeting with a positive story from a customer.

41. At Christmas, give your employees a budget of 50 Euro with which they can make customers happy. Only condition: it should be a personalised gift or surprise so the customer feels you made an effort.

42. Start each day by complimenting each other. 'Yesterday, you handled the situation with the customer very well.'

43. When someone becomes a customer, what little extra gift can you give to make them feel good right away?

44. Think for a moment how you can greet customers via mail, phone, face to face to make them feel good. What do you personally like and how can you use that in your industry?

45. Promise only what you can deliver. Organise your own success: promise something with margin that allows you to deliver faster than promised.

46. Think about 'the power of moments'. What aspect in the customer journey creates an initial peak in the relationship and how can you end with a peak at the end of the customer journey?

47. Find a way to bring customers together around a shared interest that also links back to the core of your business.

48. Activate your company's ambassadors: prompt them on how to talk about the company, involve them in decisions....

49. Involve your customers in content creation and sharing. Make it as easy and valuable as possible for customers to share content about your company.

50. Think about a way to add a positive emotion to your customer relationship.

51. Don't be afraid to give out expertise for free. Do so without any short-term expectations.

52. Provide a fast feedback system.

53. Create a feedback system that requires little effort from the customer, but provides enough info to you (e.g. Ask for NPS and one open field with the 'why?' question).

54. Provide fast action based on customer feedback: choose the simplest issues to solve first.

55. Share customer feedback with as many employees as possible in a quick and easy format.

56. Have every employee interact with real customers once every six months. Face-to-Face.

57. Organise breakfast meetings with customers to get feedback and make sure someone from a different team is there each time to get that feedback directly.

58. Start with 'Yes'. When a customer question comes in, show positive intent.

59. Experiment as much as possible with new technology. Then think about the customer benefits. Only then do you decide.

60. Provide enough customer reviews and content on the internet so that in a future with AI as gatekeeper, you will be sufficiently found by the algorithm.

61. Mirror your customers' communication channels. If the customer prefers WhatsApp, then use WhatsApp. If the customer prefers phone, you phone.

62. Do the 'click to order' test on your own site. Go to your own website and order your own products. If it is not fast enough, remove the main frictions.

63. Look at your own website via your mobile and surf to each page. Adjust the frictions.

64. Use technology only if it increases employee productivity without compromising their wellbeing.

65. See which employees naturally combine the most empathy, enthusiasm and efficiency. Let these people interact with your customers as much as possible.

66. Tell every manager in your company that they have both an operational and a cultural responsibility.

67. Organise as much valuable (inspiration, not sales) face-to-face customer contact (events, workshops, pop up stores...) as possible.

68. Monitor what is being said about your company online and organise to respond to positive or negative comments.

69. Make a list of the most common customer questions. Then create videos or articles answering those specific questions. This increases efficiency for the customer and reduces the contact centre's workload.

70. Tell your company's story through storytelling. Use the new quick interfaces and short formats to the full.

71. Be a facilitator of knowledge. Maybe you can create a podcast where you interview customers. That way, you will be seen as an industry expert and give concrete value to your customers while putting a customer in the spotlight.

72. Invest first in technology that saves the customer time.

73. If you invest in new technology, bring value to the customer, but also try to make it a PR story. Then you will have a double effect.

74. Start the day or the week with a customer experience meeting. Review the new questions and insights and link concrete action to them.

75. Make your employees' lives easier. Don't let them waste time on useless internal matters. All that time can be put into customer experience.

76. As you expand your circle of influence as a brand and speak out on some societal challenges, you will sometimes have to make choices. Be bold in doing so, like Nike with Colin Kaepernick.

77. Ensure psychological safety in your team. If something goes wrong, don't start blaming but just deal with it in a very analytical way: what went wrong and how can we avoid it?

78. Normalise dealing with mistakes. At Toyota, even on successful projects they hold a 'hansei-kai' (reflection meeting) to look at what went wrong and how to avoid it in the future. This way, you create a very open culture where mistakes are not hidden away, but dealt with.

79. Think very carefully about which KPIs you use for CX. A company that takes the number of (non-)returned products as a metric for success may cause the service team to make returning products very difficult and thus ensure very poor CX.

80. Think about how you can co-create with your customers. This not only ensures a very personalised approach, but also lets you learn a lot from what they want and expect.

81. Ask your social media network what they appreciate most about the competition and why. That is a very open way of dealing with competition and can inspire you to do better yourself.

82. Don't just use your customers' data to get smarter yourself. Make them smarter with their own data about their health, shopping behaviour, financial behaviour, etc.

83. Remember the 90% – 10% principle with technology, where it works perfectly for the 90% but leaves a lot to be desired in the latter case. Make sure your human team addresses that 10% so there is no customer frustration with a sub-optimal digital experience.

84. Try to find out what your customers are most concerned about and try to help them with that.

85. View customer-centricity as an ongoing, long-term philosophy. Sometimes you will have to hurt yourself a little in the short term to benefit yourself – together with your customer, of course – later.

86. Don't expect your customers to be loyal to you, but be loyal to your customers yourself.

87. Don't promise your customers the impossible, but be realistic. Better to promise that you will send an offer within 1.5 weeks (which is perfectly acceptable to most customers) only to send it to them after 5 days, than to say they will get it within 3 days, while they end up having to wait 5 days.

88. Give your team the chance to become 'Open Door' heroes (you know, holding that 'open door' button of a lift to help someone very altruistically with it), where they are allowed to break the rules in exceptional situations to help customers in difficult situations. That not only makes the customer feel good but also your staff.

89. Empathy should be organised as a company and structurally integrated into your business processes.

90. Train your leaders to make them aware of the impact of their micro-communications and micro-decisions. Employees watch their behaviour much more than they value their words.

91. Think about the corners of your mouth. Research how to make your customers smile. That good feeling, what I call the Top Gun Effect, is so powerful. It can sometimes happen even with very small measures such as with a funny message in a confirmation email.

92. What do you want to do: sell products or create positive change in the world? Your business needs to yield, of course, but shifting your mindset can really do wonders for your customer experience.

93. Striving for perfection can block very valuable CX ideas and experiments. Realise that customers don't want perfection, but they do want positive intent.

94. Treat your suppliers like you treat customers and employees because that will influence their output and thus indirectly impact your customers.

95. Make your services, products and interfaces fast, simple and fun: let this be your mantra in all CX changes.

96. CX starts with your talent strategy. Hire people with the right attitude: those who get genuinely excited about service and who want to give your customers great memories.

97. Take very good care of your staff because happiness is contagious. If your employees are happy, they will pass on that feeling to your customers.

98. Serendipity and chance can make shopping much more fun, research at Facebook showed. It seems counterintuitive, but I believe companies can create artificial serendipity. Netflix, for example, has a shuffle button. Birchbox sends a random selection of beauty products to customers. In a world of orchestrated customer experiences, you can stand out by encouraging such serendipity.

99. A CX strategy should be felt throughout the entire company, not just at C-level. Each individual employee should understand their role in the larger CX whole, down to what the exact impact would be if they performed their task just a little differently.

100. When Marsellus Wallace in *Pulp Fiction* had problems, he called Mr Wolf, a 'cleaner' who came to clean up the difficult problems. Who is your Mr Wolf? Who has the decisiveness and authority to sort out CX challenges with a good dose of common sense? Every company needs someone like that.

101. Create a 'Feel good mails' folder in your mailbox. Every time you get positive feedback from a customer via email, you can then put that email in that folder. On a gloomy day just scroll through those 'feel good' mails and you will have the energy to make customers happy.

102. Make it easy for your employees to be able to deliver unexpected gifts to customers once in a while. Make sure they don't have to ask permission to do so.

THANK YOU!

Writing a book is quite an adventure. The process starts with all the loose parts with inspiration and initial ideas, and it ends in a clear structure where all the ideas have their place. First comes the exploration phase, then the research phase and finally the book must be written. I personally like the latter the most. I like to write down my ideas and hope to inspire as many people as possible with them.

I have the pleasure of working with talented, enthusiastic and smart people at each of these stages. I would like to take a moment to thank them warmly.

As with my book *The Offer you Can't Refuse*, Laurence Van Elegem helped me with the research: finding cases, new metaphors and concepts. Thanks for all your efforts, Laurence!

Peter Hinssen wrote another brilliant chapter in my book. I am very happy about that. During our meetings for our RADAR (podcast) recordings, Peter always stimulates my thoughts, allowing me to start working with new insights. Thank you, Peter!

Thank you, Karl Demoen, for being the creative brain behind my content. My blogs, videos, social media posts and books would not be as impactful without your dedication and creativity. What a treat to be able to collaborate with such a creative genius. Also a lot of thanks to Joost van Lierop for his excellent making of this book.

I would like to thank the team at Lannoo Campus for their excellent cooperation. Hilde Vanmechelen, Marije Roefs, Cami Vanstapel and Niels Janssens, thank you for all the energy and expertise you put into this new book. It was once again a pleasure to work together.

Thank you to our team at Nexxworks. Julie, Eline and Matthias, you have put together a fantastic team that allows us to inspire our clients. Thanks to the hard work of everyone at Nexxworks, I can visit the most innovative regions of the world with business leaders and meet many of the international experts and companies in this book during our Nexxworks trips. I am very excited by your work, and I give a big thank you to everyone on the team.

During the first part of my career, I had the opportunity to work with truly top-notch people from whom I learned an awful lot. All these people were decisive in my career. My parents, Pol and Carine Van Belleghem, were self-employed photographers in Maldegem, Belgium. Daily, I saw how they wanted to give their customers the best possible service with a lot of commitment and respect. That is where my DNA of customer focus was born.

Professor Dr Rudy Moenaert was my first professional mentor and I still receive new insights from him every time we see each other. Always a pleasure, Rudy.

Professor Dr Marion Debruyne (Dean Vlerick School) was the first to throw me to the lions in a classroom at Vlerick. I had to learn to survive; there was nothing else to do. It was a fantastic learning experience. Today it is a pleasure to be able to regularly exchange thoughts and to learn from Marion.

I worked with Kristof De Wulf (CEO Human8) daily for 12 years. Together, we conquered new markets and convinced new customers. Kristof's drive, insights and entrepreneurial spirit helped shape me into who I am today. Thank you to my parents, Rudy, Marion and Kristof.

During my teenage years, I was lucky enough to be able to go on holiday every summer with Auntie Mieke and Uncle Ed in the San Francisco Bay Area (California, USA). There I experienced great times, but also got a taste of the spirit and positivism of Silicon Valley. There, I was able to practise the English language. It has made a huge contribution in my life. Thank you Auntie Mieke and Uncle Ed.

Thanks to you! To you! My readers. Thank you for reading this book. Thank you for engaging with all the ideas. Maybe you have been following me for some time through social media or previous books; thank you for that. The energy I get from the audience and hearing your stories makes me eager to get started every day. A big thank you.

Finally, I would like to thank my family. They are my greatest source of inspiration. Moreover, this is the first book that is truly a family project. Evi has been my first reader for more than a decade. She can formulate sentences better and sharpen ideas like the best. When I try to explain a theory in an illogical way, Evi manages to put logic into it time and again. It helps me tremendously. We have a fantastic collaboration.

This is the first book in which both our children, Siebe (14) and Mathis (12), have actively participated. Siebe inspired me to work with the metaphor of the diamond and wrote a piece of text himself for this book. I also learned about the examples about Nutella and the California Roll through Siebe. Mathis is always showing me new fun examples and videos that I can use in presentations. Thanks to Mathis, I discovered MrBeast whom I think is a brilliant example for this book and in my presentations.

Thank you, Evi, Siebe and Mathis!

Steven

PS. Thanks also to OpenAI for allowing me to use ChatGPT as a research assistant when writing this book.

NOTES

1   Survey Bain, Reichheld

2   https://cx-trends-report-2022.zendesk.com/opportunity

3   https://cx-trends-report-2022.zendesk.com/opportunity

4   https://www.reuters.com/technology/chatgpt-sets-record-fastest-gro-wing-user-base-analyst-note-2023-02-01/

5   https://www.freshworks.com/freshdesk/resources/customer-service-sta-tistics/

6   https://www.freshworks.com/freshdesk/resources/customer-service-sta-tistics/

7   https://hyken.com/2021-customer-service-customer-experience-report/

8   https://www.forbes.com/sites/shephyken/2021/08/29/customers-will-pay-more-for-this/?sh=5b5ab33416c6

9   https://www.salesforce.com/news/stories/customer-engagement-research/

10   https://screenrant.com/top-gun-maverick-2022-best-reviewed-rot-ten-tomatoes/

11   https://www.cnbc.com/2023/01/10/top-gun-maverick-disney-top-box-of-fice-2022.htm

12   The Power of Moments, Dan & Chip Heath

13   https://www.wsj.com/articles/the-hottest-app-right-now-one-where-teens-have-to-say-nice-things-about-each-other-11665940854

14   https://www.bloomberg.com/news/newsletters/2022-10-21/is-the-gas-app-free-new-social-network-is-a-hit-in-high-schools

15   https://healthypsych.com/play-strengths-science-character-strengths/

16   https://www.ncbi.nlm.nih.gov/pmc/articles/PMC4161121/

17   https://managementconsulted.com/are-optimistic-employees-more-suc-cessful/

18   https://en.wikipedia.org/wiki/Negativity_bias

19   Superbetter, by Jane McGonigal, 2016

20   https://www.technologyreview.com/2022/07/28/1056510/deepmind-pre-dicted-the-structure-of-almost-every-protein-known-to-science/

21   https://www.forbes.com/sites/abrambrown/2022/01/14/the-highest-paid-youtube-stars-mrbeast-jake-paul-and-markiplier-score-massive-pay-days/

22 https://www.latimes.com/entertainment-arts/story/2021-12-09/mr-beast-youtube-squid-game-video-hit

23 https://techcrunch.com/2022/10/25/mrbeast-1-5-billion-valuation-youtuber/

24 https://news.gallup.com/opinion/gallup/468608/young-americans-demand-businesses-solid-moral-compass.aspx

25 https://www.forbes.com/sites/deloitte/2023/01/19/from-ambition-to-impact-how-business-leaders-can-accelerate-the-green-transition/

26 https://www.bloovi.be/thema/familiebedrijven/de-circulaire-shift-van-familiebedrijf-filou-friends-voor-ons-is-dit-de-meest-logische-en-ook-enige-keuze

27 https://www.wsj.com/articles/patagonia-founder-yvon-chouinardis-giving-company-away-in-pledge-to-fight-climate-change-11663190342

28 https://www.patagonia.com/ownership/

29 https://www.youtube.com/watch?v=0j0xzuh-6rY

30 https://www.businessinsider.nl/american-kids-dream-of-being-youtube-influencers-instead-of-astronauts-2019-7?international=true&r=US

31 https://www.youtube.com/watch?v=MWdW2XbhDAM

32 https://gpseducation.oecd.org/CountryProfile?primaryCountry=IND&treshold=5&topic=EO

33 https://en.wikipedia.org/wiki/Unacademy

34 https://www.rts.com/resources/guides/food-waste-america/

35 https://www.nytimes.com/2022/03/28/business/heineken-leaving-russia-carlsberg.html

36 https://www.baysidegroup.com.au/employers/how-sustainability-can-help-employers-win-the-war-on-talent

37 https://www.pwc.com/gx/en/issues/workforce/hopes-and-fears-2022.html

38 https://www.forbes.com/sites/greatspeculations/2019/08/27/wework-is-the-most-ridiculous-ipo-of-2019/?sh=779b05861ad6

39 https://www.sme10x.com/10x-industry/how-weworks-inflated-valuation-bubble-has-burst-into-speculation-of-bankruptcy

40 https://www.qualtrics.com/uk/experience-management/customer/net-promoter-score/?rid=ip&prevsite=en&newsite=uk&geo=FR&geomatch=uk

41 https://www.scrapehero.com/location-reports/In-N-Out%20Burger-USA/

42 https://www.prnewswire.com/news-releases/in-n-out-burger-wins-con-sumer-favor-in-market-force-informations-new-study-301679727.html

43 https://www.inc.com/bill-murphy-jr/customers-just-waited-12-hours-at-in-n-out-burger-heres-big-reason-why-and-how-to-copy-it.html

44 https://books.google.be/books?id=qNVP2L6iKi0C&pg=SL3-PA36&redir_es-c=y#v=onepage&q&f=false

45 https://www.inc.com/chris-matyszczyk/in-n-out-just-closed-37-restau-rants-reason-why-is-brilliant.html

46 https://www.forbes.com/sites/chloesorvino/2018/10/10/exclusive-in-n-out-billionaire-lynsi-snyder-opens-up-about-her-troubled-past-and-the-burger-chains-future/?sh=6314afd4b9cd

47 https://www.forbes.com/sites/micahsolomon/2015/01/15/the-amazing-true-story-of-the-hotel-that-saved-thomas-the-tank-engine/?sh=1666e-d62230e

48 https://blog.vantagecircle.com/rewards-and-recognition-ideas/

49 https://www.youtube.com/watch?v=pxBQLFLei70

50 https://www.forrester.com/report/The-Customer-Emotions-Dri-ving-CX-Success/RES129194

51 https://wildalaskancompany.com/our-story

52 https://www.researchgate.net/publication/228673481_Service_Personali-zation_and_Loyalty

53 https://www.mckinsey.com/capabilities/growth-marketing-and-sales/our-insights/a-better-way-to-build-a-brand-the-community-flywheel

54 https://www.lemonde.fr/en/economy/article/2023/05/05/shein-fast-fashion-s-infernal-machine_6025510_19.html

55 https://sensortower.com/blog/shein-amazon-installs-q2-2022

56 https://kenhughes.info/consumer-collaboration-taylor-swift/

57 https://www.salesforce.com/resources/reports/state-of-the-connec-ted-customer/

58 https://www.americanexpress.com/en-us/business/trends-and-insights/articles/2017-global-customer-service-barometer/

59 https://www.mckinsey.com/capabilities/growth-marketing-and-sales/our-insights/pricing-the-next-frontier-of-value-creation-in-private-equity

60 W. Edward Deming is widely acknowledged as the leading management thinker in the field of quality. He was a statistician and business consul-

tant whose methods helped hasten Japan's recovery after the Second World War and beyond.

61 https://www.bbc.com/news/world-us-canada-63879250
62 https://www.forbes.com/sites/alistaircharlton/2021/07/28/ford-has-created-a-fragrance-designed-to-smell-like-gasoline/?sh=8179a5c5f899
63 https://www.theverge.com/2022/8/31/23318937/open-elevator-door-button-kindness
64 https://edition.cnn.com/2023/02/16/tech/temu-shopping-app-us-popularity-intl-hnk/index.html
65 https://www.ben-evans.com/presentations
66 https://www.wsj.com/articles/SB1000142405311190348090457651225091562946θ
67 https://www.mckinsey.com/featured-insights/artificial-intelligence/notes-from-the-ai-frontier-modeling-the-impact-of-ai-on-the-world-economy
68 https://www.shrm.org/executive/resources/articles/pages/age-of-ai-has-begun-bill-gates.aspx
69 https://news.mit.edu/2018/study-twitter-false-news-travels-faster-true-stories-0308
70 For an overview of how bots skew research and news see: https://www.forbes.com/sites/forbestechcouncil/2022/01/24/the-great-contamination-how-bots-and-fake-users-can-skew-an-organizations-data-and-analytics/?sh=46a145f02572
71 https://www.marubeni.com/en/research/potomac/backnumber/19.html
72 https://www.nature.com/articles/s41598-022-22856-z
73 https://deloitte.wsj.com/articles/consumers-expect-brands-to-address-climate-change-01618945334
74 https://techcrunch.com/2022/10/03/amazon-hub-affordable-shopping-options/
75 https://www.statista.com/chart/28467/virtual-and-augmented-reality-adoption-forecast/
76 US Bureau of Labor Statistics quits levels and rates data, December 2019 through May 2022.
77 https://www.mckinsey.com/capabilities/people-and-organizational-performance/our-insights/the-great-attrition-is-making-hiring-harder-are-you-searching-the-right-talent-pools

78   https://www.gallup.com/workplace/398306/quiet-quitting-real.aspx

79   https://www.hln.be/showbizz/maak-kennis-met-de-derde-meest-beluis-
      terde-vlaming-op-spotify-van-de-filipijnen-tot-amerika-overal-ter-we-
      reld-wieg-ik-mensen-in-slaap~ae9804fb/

80   https://www.tvtechnology.com/news/ampere-us-tv-households-now-
      average-four-streaming-services

81   https://www.wsj.com/articles/streaming-services-deal-with-growing-
      number-of-subscribers-who-watch-cancel-and-go-11660557601

82   https://www.wsj.com/livecoverage/stock-market-news-to-
      day-01-19-2023/card/netflix-stock-falls-ahead-of-after-hours-earn-
      ings-YfZkvZsIsRCUDLXJotMB?mod=Searchresults_pos7&page=1

ABOUT STEVEN

Steven Van Belleghem is a customer experience enthusiast! His mission is to inspire companies to become more customer-centric. Steven believes in combining common sense, new technologies, an empathic human touch, playing the long game and taking social responsibility to win the hearts and business of customers over and over again.

To achieve his mission, he has written five international bestsellers; he shares new ideas on his social channels (including his YouTube channel with more than 8 million views); he delivers keynote presentations all over the world (>1.500 keynotes in >45 countries) and his ideas are often shared by media outlets such as Forbes, The Guardian and WARC.

Steven is also an entrepreneur (co-founder of inspiration agency Nexxworks), an investor in customer experience related companies and an academic (marketing professor at the Vlerick Business School and a guest lecturer at London Business School).